LET T...
HEAR
Moses

RAY COMFORT

BRIDGE LOGOS

Newberry, FL 32669

Let Them Hear Moses:
Looking to Moses to Point People to Jesus

Published by:
Bridge-Logos
Newberry, Florida 32669, USA
bridgelogos.com

Printed in the United States of America

Library of Congress Control Number: 2019953697

ISBN 978-1-61036-217-7

Edited by Lynn Copeland

Cover, page design, and production by Genesis Group (genesis-group.net)

CONTENTS

CHAPTER One

A THICK FOREST OF FACIAL HAIR

I n the well-known parable of the Rich Man and Lazarus, Jesus gives us a glimpse of the afterlife. Though most of us are familiar with His statements about Heaven and Hell, we may have missed a surprising key to reaching our loved ones. As the rich man is begging for someone to go and testify to his family so they wouldn't end up in torment, Jesus said,

> "If they do not hear Moses and the prophets, neither will they be persuaded though one rise from the dead." (Luke 16:31)

What has Moses got to do with the gospel? After all, we are not under law, we're under grace. The law of Moses is the Old Testament; we are now in the new.

These are legitimate thoughts and questions, and there are legitimate (and biblical) answers. The moral Law (the Ten Commandments, often called the law of Moses) has everything to do with the gospel. If it wasn't for God's Law, there would be no need for the cross. Jesus suffered and died to satisfy the demands of eternal justice. If it wasn't for Moses, we wouldn't need Jesus. He saves us from the wrath of the Law. The apostle Paul said that if it wasn't for Moses, he would have had no idea of the nature of sin (see Romans 3:19,20; 7:7). Moses is as relevant to the gospel as a diagnosis is to the cure of a disease.

So let's back up a little and look closely at the life of Moses to see what we can learn from him, and then study how Moses can also be used to bring sinners to Jesus.

For past generations the name of Moses conjured up images of Charlton Heston, lost behind a thick forest of gray facial hair, with great melodrama opening the Red Sea. But there was much more to Moses than Hollywood would have us believe.

The accont of his amazing life begins in Exodus 2, when a man of the house of Levi took a wife from his own tribe and she became pregnant (vv. 1,2). Most of us began life that way. I say "most" because the one Person Moses foreshadowed was conceived when God overshadowed His mother:

> "Now the birth of Jesus Christ was as follows: After His mother Mary was betrothed to Joseph, before they came together, she was found with child of the Holy Spirit." (Matthew 1:18)

Both Moses and Jesus were Israelites by birth and began life with all the drama of an action-packed movie. Under the threat of death, Jesus was whisked away into Egypt. A paranoid King Herod had heard rumors of the promised Messiah being born and, in an insane effort to protect his throne, decided that he would cover his bases by slaughtering every male child under the age of two (see Matthew 2:16). That terrible slaughter could have been averted had he searched the Scriptures and found it was merely a harmless Lamb that was expected by Israel. This was no lionhearted conquering King—not yet.

Approximately 1,400 years earlier, Moses too was threatened in his infancy by the insecurities of a king of Egypt. After Joseph died in Egypt, his descendants "were fruitful and increased abundantly, multiplied and grew exceedingly mighty; and the land was filled with them" (Exodus 1:7). This caused a new historically ignorant king, who didn't know of Joseph or his descendants, to feel (like Herod) that his throne was threatened. He said to his people,

> "Look, the people of the children of Israel are more and mightier than we; come, let us deal shrewdly with them, lest they multiply, and it happen, in the event of war, that they also join our enemies and fight against us, and so go up out of the land." (Exodus 1:9,10)

Consequently, the Israelites were forced to become slaves in Egypt and were used to built cities for their cruel taskmasters. But the more the Egyptians afflicted them, the more they multiplied and grew, causing increasing paranoia among their afflicters:

> But the more they afflicted them, the more they multiplied and grew. And they were in dread of the children of Israel. So the Egyptians made the children of Israel serve with rigor. And they made their lives bitter with hard bondage—in mortar, in brick, and in all manner of service in the field. (Exodus 1:12–14)

In both incidents, God was invisibly at work to fulfill His purposes, and no one could thwart the purposes of God. Not Herod, and not the Egyptian Pharaoh.

Then, like godless Herod would later do, the Egyptian king decided to slaughter children. The mind boggles at such evil. Before we confine such wickedness to history, we see the same ancient demons still inspiring killers today. Rather than be overthrown by inconvenience, millions in contemporary America have slaughtered children in the womb through abortion. Nothing stands as a bloody testimony to the evil of the human heart as much as those who kill their own offspring.

> Then the king of Egypt spoke to the Hebrew midwives, of whom the name of one was Shiphrah and the name of the other Puah; and he said, "When you do the duties of a midwife for the Hebrew women, and see them on the birthstools, if it is a son, then you shall kill him; but if it is a daughter, then she shall live." (Exodus 1:15,16)

This created quite a midwife crisis. How would these women respond to such a horrendous order?

> But the midwives feared God, and did not do as the king of Egypt commanded them, but saved the male children alive. So the king of Egypt called for the midwives and said to them, "Why have you done this thing, and saved the male children alive?"
>
> And the midwives said to Pharaoh, "Because the Hebrew women are not like the Egyptian women; for they are lively and give birth before the midwives come to them." (Exodus 1:17–19)

AN IMPORTANT POINT

In this short passage we see an answer to a loaded question often thrown at us by skeptics. They say,

> "You are in Germany in 1941. The Nazis come to your home and ask if there are any Jews in the building. You are hiding a Jewish family behind a false wall upstairs. Do you lie to them and sin against your God, or do you

tell the truth and let the Nazis know where they are hiding?"

There is another aspect to telling the truth to the Nazis. In doing so, I would be helping their cause by informing on the whereabouts of Jews (in this case, my loved ones). If I knew that my neighbors were also hiding Jews in their home, if asked, should I tell the truth about their location? Should I become an informant, and give aid to the enemy?

If I were a soldier, should I help the enemy by giving him the truth when asked for sensitive military information? If I did so, I would be considered a traitor. Would that also be the case if I considered myself a soldier in a battle against evil, by being part of the resistance and hiding Jews?

Like the skeptics, the Pharisees often tried to create "Aha!" scenarios for Jesus, hoping to trap Him in His speech. But they never did:

> Then they sent to Him some of the Pharisees and the Herodians, to catch Him in His words. When they had come, they said to Him, "Teacher, we know that You are true, and care about no one; for You do not regard the person of men, but teach the way of God in truth. Is it lawful to pay taxes to Caesar, or not? Shall we pay, or shall we not pay?"
>
> But He, knowing their hypocrisy, said to them, "Why do you test Me? Bring Me a denarius that I may see it." So they brought it.
>
> And He said to them, "Whose image and inscription is this?" They said to Him, "Caesar's."
>
> And Jesus answered and said to them, "Render to Caesar the things that are Caesar's, and to God the things that are God's."

And they marveled at Him. (Mark 12:13–17)

We know that they were insincere by Jesus' reaction to the question. He said, "Why do you test Me?" And He obviously didn't lie. He simply outwitted their wickedness.

However, the midwives didn't have divine wit; they outright lied to the Egyptian king. But Scripture tells us that they lied to him *because* they feared God. They chose to not tell the truth rather than be a party to the murder of babies. And we don't have to guess what God's response was to this supposed sin:

> *Therefore* God dealt well with the midwives, and the people multiplied and grew very mighty. (Exodus 1:20)

The midwives feared God and refused the king's command. How could anyone who feared the Lord be a party to the murder of Jews, or of innocent children? And there lies the problem with modern America. We have lost the fear of God, and when that precious virtue is removed, the dam of evil eventually bursts onto any nation.

The cracks had been growing for a long time, but they became larger just after the Second World War when thoughts of God were exchanged for an idol. With the threat of the evil of Nazi domination suddenly gone, many believed divine protection was no longer needed. The restraint of Hollywood's Hays Code, governing morality in movies, was removed in the 1960s and sin flooded a generation.

The world found their freedom from restraint in the sexual revolution of the 1950 and 1960s. In the following generations the fear of God eventually became a despised doctrine. But it is the fear of God to which we must return—not to get America on its feet, but to get it on its knees. The gospel is only for the humble (James 4:6), and unregenerate humanity will never be humbled until it fears God. To fear Him is the beginning of wisdom.

Those God-fearing midwives who didn't fear the king put themselves in danger to save human lives. And if we fear God, we will do all we can to stop the holocaust of abortion in America.

When I have questioned college students about a woman's right to take the life of her unborn child, many, knowing full well that it is a baby in the womb, still condone killing for convenience. Moving goalposts, not being honest, or being unreasonable isn't confined to the issue of abortion.

Skeptics (especially atheists) dream up scenarios to argue about, not because they care about truth, but because they love their sins. If they can disprove the Bible or trip us up with questions, in their minds they have us conquered. Their questions are often statements: "Who made God?" or "Why is there suffering?" They don't think we have an answer. Neither do they want an answer, and they walk away thinking they have won the game.

IT IS THE FEAR OF GOD TO WHICH WE MUST RETURN— NOT TO GET AMERICA ON ITS FEET, BUT TO GET IT ON ITS KNEES.

When the Pharisees asked Jesus if an adulterous women should be stoned for her sin, they thought that they had put Him between a rock and a hard place (see John 8:3–11). But Jesus turned the rock toward them. They too were sinners and had to face the same Law of Moses that they were seeking to use to condemn the woman. And in that wonderful narrative we have the soul-stirring story of God's amazing mercy toward sinners. Each of the accusers went away accused by Moses, but only God knows how many of those men eventually stood with penitent hearts at the foot of the cross as the Savior suffered for their sins.

More often than not we can turn these scenarios into opportunities to testify about the mercy of God. Just give their question the best answer you have and then share the gospel. It's the gospel that has the promised power (see Romans 1:16) and not your answer. When the accusing religious leaders hounded a blind man whose eyes had been miraculously opened by the Savior, the man didn't argue about whether Jesus was sinless. He simply testified to what He had done:

> So they again called the man who was blind, and said to him, "Give God the glory! We know that this Man is a sinner."
>
> He answered and said, "Whether He is a sinner or not I do not know. One thing I know: that though I was blind, now I see." (John 9:24,25)

There are ways to answer difficult questions without falling into the set trap. Take, for example, the question of the exclusivity of Christianity. That is normally a difficult question. Surely saying that Jesus is the only way to God is arrogant, intolerant, and even hateful, isn't it? If we are not wise in our words, it can sound as though it is. The key is to answer the question with patience and with sound doctrine.

The way to do that with this question is to sympathetically show that all humanity has a big problem: death.

Death is cold, hard, and irrefutable evidence that God is serious about the issue of sin. Death is our terrifying and earned wages (see Romans 6:23). Without a Savior to save us, our last breath will be breathtakingly frightening. The question we must ask the unsaved is, "What are you doing to prepare yourself for this, your biggest moment in life? And what are you doing to prepare yourself for what comes after death?"

If the world thinks dying is a problem, after death they will have an even bigger problem: the judgment. Most of the world's religions believe that there will be a Day of Judgment, but they believe the way to fix the problem of sin is with good works. They have sinned against God but think they can balance the scales with religious deeds, such as good works, prayer, penance, fasting, etc. But that won't even work in a court of law with an earthly judge. A good judge will consider the crime committed, not any good deeds done by the criminal, especially if they were done with the intent of swaying the judge's mind about the crime—"I raped and murdered that woman, but look at how much money I just gave to charity."

Such a pathetic attempt to bribe the judge would bring nothing but wrath from the bench. And so it is with God. He will not be swayed to pervert justice by our good works, our giving to charity, sitting on hard pews, praying at certain times each day, etc. Nothing can save guilty sinners from the demands of Eternal Justice but the mercy of God. And that was extended only in the suffering death of Jesus Christ.

These religions rely on human sacrificial works to try to earn salvation. However, in the gospel we see that the necessary sacrifice was made by God Himself, *and that's good news for the whole of humanity*, whether they be Hindu, Muslim, Buddhist, churchgoer, atheist, or agnostic. The gospel is a universal invitation to guilty sinners to be cleansed of sin, to escape the terror of Hell, and to find absolute assurance of immortality and eternal pleasure. If you are a skeptic, jump without a parachute, stand on your own oxygen hose, but please, oh please, don't be so foolish as to damn yourself by creating silly scenarios to reject the gospel and hinder your own eternal salvation.

The Egyptian midwives' choice to lie rather than to murder (and be blessed by God for doing that) shows us that our Creator is reasonable in the truest sense of the word. The Judge takes into account extenuating circumstances.

The first chapter of Exodus then ends with a terrifying decree from Egypt's paranoid leader demanding that everyone participate in his murderous plot:

> So Pharaoh commanded all his people, saying, "Every son who is born you shall cast into the river, and every daughter you shall save alive." (Exodus 1:22)

Here begins a real-life scenario that reveals a glimmer of the omniscient mind of God. He knew what was about to take place in Egypt, and He was of course ready. There are times when I think about the divine omniscience—that God knows, sees, and hears everything. How could that be? I can only register one or two thoughts at once. If someone talks to me when I'm writing or watching news, I lose my train of thought. It's completely derailed. So when I think of God having trillions upon trillions of thoughts at the same time, my mind implodes. That thought vanishes because it's too much for my tiny brain and I find refuge in the words of the psalmist:

> O LORD, You have searched me and known me.
> You know my sitting down and my rising up;
> You understand my thought afar off.
> You comprehend my path and my lying down,

And are acquainted with all my ways.
For there is not a word on my tongue,
But behold, O LORD, You know it altogether.
You have hedged me behind and before,
And laid Your hand upon me.
Such knowledge is too wonderful for me;
It is high, I cannot attain it. (Psalm 139:1–6)

While Pharaoh was plotting his genocide, God was overruling his evil plan with a plan of His own.

BEAUTIFUL BABE

In Exodus chapter 2 we are told of Moses' birth. Every mother, no matter how ugly her newborn, thinks the baby is beautiful, but this one truly was (v. 3), and because he was a male and therefore in danger of his life, she hid him for three months. But you can only hide a baby for so long. As infants grow bigger, so do their lungs, and their cries can become louder than an airbus in full throttle. So his mother, in an effort to save her precious child from being slaughtered by the Egyptians, put him in a mini-ark and launched him into the hands of God. We pick up the story from Scripture:

> Then the daughter of Pharaoh came down to bathe at the river. And her maidens walked along the riverside; and when she saw the ark among the reeds, she sent her maid to get it. And when she opened it, she saw the child, and behold, the baby wept. So she had compassion on him, and said, "This is one of the Hebrews' children."
>
> Then his sister said to Pharaoh's daughter, "Shall I go and call a nurse for you from the Hebrew women, that she may nurse the child for you?"
>
> And Pharaoh's daughter said to her, "Go." So the maiden went and called the child's mother. Then Phar-

11

aoh's daughter said to her, "Take this child away and nurse him for me, and I will give you your wages." So the woman took the child and nursed him. And the child grew, and she brought him to Pharaoh's daughter, and he became her son. So she called his name Moses, saying, "Because I drew him out of the water." (Exodus 2:5–10)

This ark's maiden voyage had titanic consequences because Almighty God had condescended to fulfill His plans through a young girl. In using Moses' sister, He was delivering Israel's deliverer into the hands of the very one who had given him up: his mother. That is so often the way God works. If we give up something to God, He often gives it back with extras. He gives it back better, leaving our limited human minds boggling at His love and infinite ability. He let Lazarus die, and then presented him alive to his mourners. He allowed Jesus to be crucified and then presented Him alive three days later to His unbelieving disciples. God's ways are beyond understanding:

> HE WAS DELIVERING ISRAEL'S DELIVERER INTO THE HANDS OF THE VERY ONE WHO HAD GIVEN HIM UP: HIS MOTHER.

Oh, the depth of the riches both of the wisdom and knowledge of God! How unsearchable are His judgments and His ways past finding out!

"For who has known the mind of the LORD?
Or who has become His counselor?"
"Or who has first given to Him
And it shall be repaid to him?"

> For of Him and through Him and to Him are all things, to whom be glory forever. Amen. (Romans 11:33–36)

God deeply cared for the mother of Moses, for his sweet sister, and for the nation of Israel, and He cared for you and me *way back in the annals of time.* He saved baby Moses so that through him He could save the children of Israel, so that through their descendants He could send the Messiah to save you and me from death and Hell. He had us in mind way back then.

The reason the mother of Moses entrusted God with her son was that she feared for his death. And consequently the daughter of Pharaoh adopted him and guaranteed his life. Moses' mom was then given back her beloved son and was even paid to raise him as a child of the Pharaoh himself. Who in their wildest dreams could have thought that such a thing would happen? But it did, and you and I can step into that same realm of the miraculous, if we also trust God. No matter what life throws at us, we have this immutable promise:

> And we know that all things work together for good to those who love God, to those who are the called according to His purpose. (Romans 8:28)

The moment we let go of our safe plans and abandon ourselves to "Not my will, but Yours be done," we can stand on that precious promise. It is ours because we are then "called according to His purpose." It becomes ours in Christ. This promise is the brightest of lights in the darkest of times. It's even more than that. It's there as a light when there's no natural light at the end of the tunnel. That means we can have a steadfast hope in the lion's den. It is in that promise that we see His loving hand, and can say with Paul,

Who shall separate us from the love of Christ? Shall tribulation, or distress, or persecution, or famine, or nakedness, or peril, or sword? As it is written:

"For Your sake we are killed all day long;
We are accounted as sheep for the slaughter."

Yet in all these things we are more than conquerors through Him who loved us. For I am persuaded that neither death nor life, nor angels nor principalities nor powers, nor things present nor things to come, nor height nor depth, nor any other created thing, shall be able to separate us from the love of God which is in Christ Jesus our Lord. (Romans 8:35–39)

WAS IT PREMEDITATED MURDER?

Scripture leaves us in the dark about the youth of Moses. Neither do we know anything about the youth of Jesus—other than the famous incident when He was twelve and His parents unwittingly left Him in Jerusalem. We are told that when they found Him,

He said to them, "Why did you seek Me? Did you not know that I must be about My Father's business?" But they did not understand the statement which He spoke to them.

Then He went down with them and came to Nazareth, and was subject to them, but His mother kept all these things in her heart. And Jesus increased in wisdom and stature, and in favor with God and men. (Luke 2:49–52)

Jesus was without sin, because He was divine. But not so with Moses. It is evident that, like the rest of the sons and daughters of Adam, sin ran like a river in the blood of Moses.

When he reached manhood, Moses saw an Egyptian beating a Hebrew, and he killed him. Scripture says that before Moses did this "he looked this way and that way, and when he saw no one, he killed the Egyptian and hid him in the sand" (Exodus 2:12).

Taking the life of another human being would seem to have been premeditated. Then Moses buried the body in an effort to cover his crime. A God-fearing man doesn't look "this way and that way." He looks toward the heavens. His actions are governed by the knowledge that God's holy eyes see everything. He is a witness to our every thought and deed. It seems that Moses let sin come through the door; anger blinded his reason.

There is, however, another thought. Perhaps this wasn't premeditated murder, because he didn't intend to kill the Egyptian. Perhaps his looking "this way and that way" was because, as an Egyptian, he simply didn't want to be seen defending a Hebrew slave—giving aid and comfort to the enemy.

Later on in Scripture we see that God's Word distinguishes between premeditated murder, *which was given the death penalty* (Exodus 21:12–14) and someone who *accidentally* killed another person (Exodus 21:13). Whatever the case with Moses, God used him despite that incident.

We need not concern ourselves with the vessels God chooses to do His bidding. He chose to use Saul of Tarsus, who in rage took the lives of Jesus' followers, and Moses who took the life of an Egyptian. God doesn't make mistakes or make bad choices. He chooses sinful men and women to do His will, because none of us in the Adamic race is without sin. Each of us can look back at our lives before our burning bush encounter, or our road to Damascus experience, and see a different person. We were once ruled by our sinful passions. But God was rich in mercy, and in retrospect, we can even see His merciful hand guiding us before we came to the cross. We, like Moses, thought we had buried our sin and that there were no witnesses. But Scripture informed us that all things are naked and open before the eyes of God (Hebrews 4:13).

The day after Moses took the life of the Egyptian, he saw two Hebrews fighting, and he said to the one who did the wrong, "Why are you striking your companion?" Then the man replied, "Who made you a prince and a judge over us? Do you intend to kill me as you killed the Egyptian?" (Exodus 2:13,14).

There had been a witness:

> So Moses feared and said, "Surely this thing is known!" When Pharaoh heard of this matter, he sought to kill Moses. But Moses fled from the face of Pharaoh and dwelt in the land of Midian; and he sat down by a well. (Exodus 2:14,15)

While we are not sure exactly when Moses came to faith —when he refused Egypt's pleasures and trusted in God— we do know that this happened "when he became of age":

> By faith Moses, when he became of age, refused to be called the son of Pharaoh's daughter, choosing rather to suffer affliction with the people of God than to enjoy the passing pleasures of sin, esteeming the reproach of Christ greater riches than the treasures in Egypt; for he looked to the reward. (Hebrews 11:24–26)

No doubt the seeds of godly influence sown by his faithful mother grew as Moses grew. The pleasurable sins of

Egypt never fully extinguished the light of conscience in Moses. He chose to deny himself, because he saw Him who is invisible (Hebrews 11:27).

THE DAILY BATTLE

As Christians, we choose daily to deny ourselves the pleasures of sin. The eyes, the ears, the mind, and the very heart of our sinful nature are attracted to Egypt's titillating pleasures. Lust, the pride of life, tantalizing gossip, the sparkling lure of money, and a thousand other evils promise endless pleasure. But we refuse to serve the devil because his wages are but nothing but a dirty drain's deadly dregs compared to the endless pure water of life:

WE, LIKE MOSES, THOUGHT WE HAD BURIED OUR SIN AND THAT THERE WERE NO WITNESSES.

> And he showed me a pure river of water of life, clear as crystal, proceeding from the throne of God and of the Lamb. In the middle of its street, and on either side of the river, was the tree of life, which bore twelve fruits, each tree yielding its fruit every month. The leaves of the tree were for the healing of the nations. And there shall be no more curse, but the throne of God and of the Lamb shall be in it, and His servants shall serve Him. They shall see His face, and His name shall be on their foreheads. There shall be no night there: They need no lamp nor light of the sun, for the Lord God gives them light. And they shall reign forever and ever. (Revelation 22:1–5)

We have far greater riches in Christ. We don't live by a blind faith as the world so often says, but we have entered into a living trust when we are partakers of the divine nature, because that's the means to our inheritance. We have riches that will never fade.

Choosing to follow Jesus is a calculated decision. It is reasonable in the truest sense of the word. We choose life over death, Heaven over Hell, glorious light instead of darkness, and everlasting pleasure rather than terrible pain. Choosing to follow the Savior is reasonable, sensible, and sane. It is the same calculation that brought the Prodigal Son to his senses (see Luke 15). He could choose to stay and starve in the stinking pigsty, or he could choose to return to his father.

Choosing Christianity over the pleasures of this world is a no-brainer, as we will continue to see in the next chapter.

CHAPTER Two

A NEW LEAF

I n Luke chapter 5, we see the famous incident of Jesus calling Peter, James, and John as His disciples. They had been fishing all night and had caught nothing. That's nothing new for those who fish. While modern professional fishermen use sounding devices to locate large shoals of fish, the rest of us are left to guess where they are, or pray that we get at least one face-saving fish to take back home. But in this passage Jesus said, "Launch out into the deep and let down your nets for a catch" (v. 4). He didn't say to let down their nets for another attempt to catch some fish. He was specific, telling them to let down their nets for a "catch."

Simon Peter was understandably skeptical. He protested, "Master, we have toiled all night and caught nothing; nevertheless at Your word I will let down the net" (v. 5). Peter did as Jesus said, and to the astonishment of the fishermen, they caught a "great number of fish"—so many that their net began to break. And when they emptied their nets into two boats, the boats began to sink.

Here was a small fortune in sales. But instead of seeing dollar signs, Simon Peter "fell down at Jesus' knees, saying, 'Depart from me, for I am a sinful man, O Lord!'" (v. 8). It seems he had the revelation that only God can tell fish what to do. These weren't a group of dolphins that Jesus had previously spent years training, so that they would respond to a command. These were fish that no human eye had seen, swimming deep within the water, when suddenly the hand of the Maker steered them into the net. Therefore, Jesus was certainly who He said He was—the Christ, the Son of the living God. The second influence that brought Peter to his knees was no doubt the words of Jesus. Earlier in the chapter, we are told He taught the multitude from Peter's boat:

> So it was, as the multitude pressed about Him to hear the word of God, that He stood by the Lake of Gennesaret, and saw two boats standing by the lake; but the fishermen had gone from them and were washing their nets. Then He got into one of the boats, which was Simon's, and asked him to put out a little from the land. And He sat down and taught the multitudes from the boat. (Luke 5:1–3)

As Peter knelt before Jesus, He said to him,

> "Do not be afraid. From now on you will catch men." So when they had brought their boats to land, they forsook all and followed Him. (vv. 10,11)

They left their boats. They left the fortune of fresh fish, their families, and their own plans to follow Jesus. Why? Because they had found the way to everlasting life. And there is nothing more precious. That's the revelation this dying world must come to, so that they too will want to follow Jesus. How our heart leaps for joy when one sinner begins to understand what we have in Christ. Following are two wonderful comments from our YouTube channel. The first is from a woman named Danielle who had just watched our pro-life documentary "7 Reasons":

> This is THE first time I've ever cried (quietly flowing down my cheeks and dripping off my chin kinda tears) regarding the abortion I had 9 years ago. I've LITERALLY NEVER felt convicted not once before...I've just sat here frowning, now my eyes have dried, and thinking to myself, "Wow, what IS happening to me?!"...I'm a feminist, pro-choice (I thought), equality, love and peace to all kinda person. I guess I better think again. Mind = blown. Thank you for this video.

After I contacted her, her next comment ended with "and have a blessed day." No big deal for most, but for Danielle to say that was an encouraging sign.

The second comment is from a scientist named Chris:

> I used to be an atheist until last year. I used to think you Christians were crazy nuts. Turns out you guys are actually much smarter and way too stubborn to give up. That made me interested on the why rather than the how. I worked in a Darwinian science group in my university. I began to doubt Darwinism after we published some experiments at the Smithsonian. I am not a Christian but I will gladly say I am a full Theist now.

I responded by thanking him for being open and asking for his thoughts on another of our movies, "Crazy Bible."[1] After watching it he responded:

> Good movie. Really makes me rethink my stance on all of this. Perhaps I should understand better what makes you Christians so adamant on this. Maybe I was wrong on how I see you. I deeply apologize. For now that's all I

can say but I say it firmly and honestly. Specially when that man said, "There is nothing and nothingness" and later tried to explain it with reason (big fail). That actually made me reflect on how crazy some ideas in science can be. Kinda hurts since I am a scientist.

Two days later he wrote:

Hey Mr. Comfort and all of you in Living Waters. Hope you remember me. I was the forensic scientist who became a Theist not too long ago. I began to read the Bible this morning after some kind people replied on my last comment. It's still hard to swallow since I was atheist for so long but I am starting to see why my friend and you Christians see inspiration in these Scriptures…

BACK TO MOSES

With Pharaoh seeking to kill him, Moses fled for his life from Egypt into the land of Midian. As he approached a well, he saw seven maidens whose father was the priest of Midian. They had gathered at the well to draw water for their father's flock:

Then the shepherds came and drove them away; but Moses stood up and helped them, and watered their flock. When they came to Reuel their father, he said, "How is it that you have come so soon today?" And they said, "An Egyptian delivered us from the hand of the shepherds, and he also drew enough water for us and watered the flock." So he said to his daughters, "And where is he? Why is it that you have left the man? Call him, that he may eat bread." (Exodus 2:17–20)

The daughters were mistaken. Moses may have *looked* like an Egyptian, but he wasn't. He was born a Hebrew.

How mistaken the world is about Jesus of Nazareth. He may look as though He was of this world, but after a little research into His words we are forced into another conclusion. Some believe He was merely a prophet, or an interesting historical figure, while others think He was just a great teacher. There are some who believe He was a trickster, a conman, the greatest deceiver of all time, because two thousand years after He lived, millions (if not billions) live for Him and follow His teachings.

The conclusion for those who follow the evidence is that He was indeed God manifest in human form:

And without controversy great is the mystery of godliness:

God was manifested in the flesh,
Justified in the Spirit,
Seen by angels,
Preached among the Gentiles,
Believed on in the world,
Received up in glory. (1 Timothy 3:16)

It is an eye-opening and breathtaking revelation to know that the atoms in the eyes that you are using at the moment —and the trillions of brain cells that are processing your thoughts—were made by Jesus of Nazareth. In speaking of Him, Scripture says:

In the beginning was the Word, and the Word was with God, and the Word was God. He was in the beginning with God. *All things were made through Him, and without Him nothing was made that was made.* (John 1:1–3)

All things were made by Him. Without Him nothing was made. Every atom in the universe was shaped by His Word.

In speaking of Jesus being the Creator, the Bible uses the words "all things" again:

> He is the image of the invisible God, the firstborn over all creation. For by Him *all things were created* that are in heaven and that are on earth, visible and invisible, whether thrones or dominions or principalities or powers. *All things were created through Him and for Him.* (Colossians 1:15,16)

Moses was also thought to be an Egyptian by Reuel, a priest from Midian. The Midianites were the descendants of Midian, who was a son of Abraham and his wife Keturah (Genesis 25:1,2). Moses seemed to be from a nation that oppressed his people, but Reuel (also called Jethro) still welcomed him into his home with Middle Eastern hospitality.

THIS WORLD ISN'T OUR HOME. WE ARE SICKENED BY ITS EVIL, AND WE LONG FOR THE KINGDOM TO COME.

And so in a country far from his Egyptian past, Moses began a new life. He turned over a new leaf as he settled with the Midianites. He was now content with life, presumably because he was with his own people:

> Then Moses was content to live with the man, and he gave Zipporah his daughter to Moses. And she bore him a son. He called his name Gershom, for he said, "I have been a stranger in a foreign land." (Exodus 2:21,22)

Becoming a Christian is more than turning over a fresh new leaf. We become a brand new fruit-bearing tree. It's more than changing clothes, countries, or a lifestyle, or having

New Year's resolutions, or cleaning up our life because of a miserable past.

We are new creatures in Christ so that we become strangers to this world:

> Beloved, *I beg you as sojourners and pilgrims*, abstain from fleshly lusts which war against the soul, having your conduct honorable among the Gentiles, that when they speak against you as evildoers, they may, by your good works which they observe, glorify God in the day of visitation. (1 Peter 2:11,12)

This world isn't our home. We are sickened by its evil, and we long for the Kingdom to come: "For here we have no continuing city, but we seek the one to come" (Hebrews 13:14). This happens because we have been born again. Before we entered this world we were confined to the darkness of our mother's womb, but through the miracle of natural birth we began a new life. We look back on the darkness of our unsaved state and see a helpless and hopeless creature, who lived in darkness until God opened the eyes of our understanding through the gospel. When we repented and trusted in Christ, we experienced the new birth.

In reference to this new birth, this thoughtful comment was left on our YouTube channel:

> I've got a very serious question: HOW do you TRUST in Jesus? I'm raised a Christian but I know I'm not born again. I always heard that we do not want to be children of God ("There is no one who seeks God. All have turned away"). In our church we are very cautious of just accepting Jesus, because you cannot do that yourself: it's 100% mercy, God has to do 100%, you can't just decide in a moment like "I'm accepting Jesus." That doesn't

work: God has to do it. But I can't do anything now but pray and read the Bible, and I'm kind of still waiting until I'm born again. You would genuinely give people from my church a scare if you would tell them to "Just trust in Jesus" (they'd think you're a Jesus-hippie-freak).

So: is my church wrong? Where does the Bible say to trust in Jesus and you'll be fine? What do I do except for trying not to sin, reading the Bible and praying? I don't feel like I can change my heart. I can in decision-making but not as in that the core of my being wants to live for God. A few days later I'll have other priorities again. I would appreciate it if you (or someone else) would answer this. Thank you for all your videos! God bless.

The Bible never tells us to "accept" Jesus; it calls all men to respond to the gospel message by obeying God's command to *repent* and *believe*. While it is true that salvation is of the Lord (Psalm 3:8; Psalm 62:1) and that He grants repentance to the acknowledging of the truth (2 Timothy 2:25), God doesn't do the repenting. *We* do. Evidence that we are the ones who exercise repentance is that He *commands* us to do so:

> "Truly, these times of ignorance God overlooked, *but now commands all men everywhere to repent*, because He has appointed a day on which He will judge the world in righteousness by the Man whom He has ordained. He has given assurance of this to all by raising Him from the dead." (Acts 17:30,31)

Lazarus was brought to life by Jesus, but he had to get up and get out of the stinking tomb. Jesus said in a loud voice, "Lazarus, *come forth!*" (John 11:43). What a fool he would have been to ignore that command and instead lie in the cold tomb and starve to death. Jesus said, "*Come to Me*, all you who labor and are heavy laden..." (Matthew 11:28). He commands, and we respond. To do nothing is to be foolish, stay in your sins, under His wrath, justly heading for Hell.

The sinner is on the road of sin with the fully laden eighteen-wheeler of God's Law heading for him, and it will grind him to powder if he stays on the road (see Matthew 21:44). Our urgent message to all humanity is to get off the road of sin—to flee from the wrath to come. They are not to wait for some nebulous feeling issuing out of bad theology. God's command for all mankind to repent comes from His desire for our well-being. It doesn't take a genius to think this through. Life is better than death. Heaven is better than Hell. Pleasure is better than pain. God is "not willing that any should perish but that *all* should come to repentance" (2 Peter 3:9). Jesus said that "unless you repent you will all likewise perish" (Luke 13:3).

THE STUMBLING BLOCK OF FAITH

Now to the second part of this person's question: "Where does the Bible say to trust in Jesus and you'll be fine?"

There is much confusion in the world as to the meaning of faith. It's often translated in the Bible as the word "believe." When I ask someone if he *believes* in God, I'm asking a twofold question. The first part is, *does he believe that God created the universe?* I already know the answer to this question, but I ask him to bring out the important point that every human being intuitively believes in the existence of the Creator. The heavens *declare* the glory of God. They loudly herald His existence:

For the wrath of God is revealed from heaven against all ungodliness and unrighteousness of men, who suppress the truth in unrighteousness, because what may be known of God is manifest in them, for God has shown it to them. For since the creation of the world His invisible attributes are clearly seen, being understood by the things that are made, even His eternal power and Godhead, *so that they are without excuse.* (Romans 1:18–20)

The second meaning of *faith* is something that's more important to drive home into the sinner's mind. It means to have an implicit trust. We not only want him to believe in God intellectually, but we want him to *trust* in Jesus for his eternal salvation. Jesus said, "Let not your heart be troubled; you believe in God, believe also in Me" (John 14:1).

Here are the two meanings together in Scripture:

But without faith it is impossible to please Him, for he who comes to God must *believe that He is*, and that *He is a rewarder of those who diligently seek Him.* (Hebrews 11:6)

The Greek word used here for "faith" is *pistis* (a noun) and the word for "believe" is *pisteuō* (a verb). Both of these words in Greek can mean "believe, depend, obey, trust, or assurance." So in the original language of John 3:16 (when Scripture is saying that whoever *believes* in Jesus will not perish but have everlasting life), it is saying that anyone who depends on or trusts in Him will not perish. Here is the verse from the Amplified Bible:

For God so [greatly] loved and dearly prized the world, that He [even] gave His [One and] only begotten Son, so that whoever believes and trusts in Him [as Savior] shall not perish, but have eternal life.

When we believe in Jesus we are trusting in Him as our personal sin-bearer and deliverer from death. The moment we truly repent and trust in Him, we are made a new creation in Christ. Old things pass away, and all things become new (see 2 Corinthians 5:17). This is not at all like what happens with a New Year's resolution, or a new attitude, or, as with Moses, a new country.

STRANGER IN A FOREIGN LAND

As we saw, Moses named his son Gershom (Exodus 18:2,3), which means "a stranger there." Moses thought of himself as a stranger in a foreign land—perhaps a reference to his life in Egypt where he longed to be with his Hebrew people. As Christians, we groan within ourselves for the coming Kingdom (2 Corinthians 5:1,2). This God-hating world isn't our home. But there is another groan within our hearts:

> Now it happened in the process of time that the king of Egypt died. Then the children of Israel groaned because of the bondage, and they cried out; and their cry came up to God because of the bondage. So God heard their groaning, and God remembered His covenant with Abraham, with Isaac, and with Jacob. And God looked upon the children of Israel, and God acknowledged them. (Exodus 2:23–25)

The unsaved surround us. They are in terrible bondage to sin and death, having been taken captive by the devil to do his will (2 Timothy 2:26). And he is a cruel taskmaster.

Before I was a Christian I was a slave to sin and death. But the moment I was liberated, I was overwhelmed with a groan. It was an impassioned cry for unsaved human beings who were still in bondage to "Egypt." Multitudes were justly heading for Hell.

This is because one dark night, many years ago, in my lost state I cried out in anguish. Tears rolled down my cheeks as I thought about the great issues of life and death. It took a little time for the revelation to fully weigh on me, but that night I faced the truth. I was hopelessly chained to death. I couldn't understand why I was helpless before this terror that so loomed before me, it took my breath away. Hebrews 2:14,15 give details of my plight:

> Inasmuch then as the children have partaken of flesh and blood, He Himself likewise shared in the same, that through death He might destroy him who had the power of death, that is, the devil, and release those who through fear of death were all their lifetime subject to bondage.

That night, as tears of anguish streamed down my face, I cried out, "Why? Why are we born to die?" The beautiful bubble of life (when burst by the sharp pin of death) may as well not even exist. It is vanity. All is vanity. Senseless chasing of the wind. When I cried out that night, God heard my cry and delivered me from my terrifying bondage. It is that experience that is a continuous empathetic catalyst for my concern for the lost.

In an article titled "Why Doris Day Will Have 'No Funeral, No Memorial and No Marker': 'She Didn't Like Death,'" *People* magazine said,

> Doris Day won't be having a funeral after she died at the age of 97. The legendary Hollywood star, who died on Monday morning, made her wishes clear in her will, her manager and close friend Bob Bashara tells *People*.

"No funeral, no memorial and no [grave] marker," Bashara says.

In addition to saying Day didn't "like to talk about" a prospective funeral or memorial, Bashara explains, "She didn't like death, and she couldn't be with her animals if they had to be put down. She had difficulty accepting death."

"She believed in God, and she thought her voice was God-given," he says. "She would say, 'God gave me a voice, and I just used it.'"[2]

When I read this, my heart ached. I groaned within because it isn't "news" that the poor woman "didn't like death" and that she had trouble accepting it. *No one likes death*. No one gracefully accepts it. No one in their right mind, that is. Sane people are terrified by it. We recoil in horror, because no one wants to die!

I was saved from death because back in time, God heard the groaning of the offspring of Adam, and in

WHEN I CRIED OUT THAT NIGHT, GOD HEARD MY CRY AND DELIVERED ME FROM MY TERRIFYING BONDAGE.

His great kindness raised up a Deliverer. A Savior. The Scriptures heralded this coming Deliverer eight centuries years before His appearance in Bethlehem as a Babe in a manger:

> The people who walked in darkness
> Have seen a great light;
> Those who dwelt in the land of the shadow of death,
> Upon them a light has shined . . .
> For unto us a Child is born,
> Unto us a Son is given;

And the government will be upon His shoulder.
And His name will be called
Wonderful, Counselor, Mighty God,
Everlasting Father, Prince of Peace. (Isaiah 9:2,6)

God was manifest in human form:

In the beginning was the Word, and the Word was with
God, and the Word was God...And the Word became
flesh and dwelt among us, and we beheld His glory, the
glory as of the only begotten of the Father, full of grace
and truth. (John 1:1,14)

And now, we who have escaped the bondage of this sinful world and the power of death, groan to see the earth's
captives set free.

CHAPTER Three

MOSES, THE SHEPHERD

Moses' father-in-law, Jethro, had his own flock of sheep to provide wool for clothing and meat for food. In gaining a son-in-law in Moses, he also gained a shepherd for his sheep.

> Now Moses was tending the flock of Jethro his father-in-law, the priest of Midian. And he led the flock to the back of the desert, and came to Horeb, the mountain of God. And the Angel of the LORD appeared to him in a flame of fire from the midst of a bush. So he looked, and behold, the bush was burning with fire, but the bush was not consumed. Then Moses said, "I will now turn aside and see this great sight, why the bush does not burn." (Exodus 3:1–3)

Life for the ungodly is nothing but the back of a desert. Until we encounter God through the cross, we live a dry, futile, and lifeless existence. Time, like the burning heat of the desert sun, will soon take its toll. The rich and poor, strong and weak, tall and short, the wise and the fool all die. From our youth, demons, like hungry vultures, fly around our godless head. In the last chapter, we saw from the book of Hebrews that we are haunted by the fear of death *all of our lifetime*. Look at that same verse in the Amplified Bible:

> Therefore, since [these His] children share in flesh and blood [the physical nature of mankind], He Himself in a similar manner also shared in the same [physical nature, but without sin], so that through [experiencing] death He might make powerless (ineffective, impotent) him who had the power of death—that is, the devil—and [that He] might free all those who through [the haunting] fear of death were held in slavery throughout their lives. (Hebrews 2:14,15, AMP)

When I came to the cross, I was set free from the bondage of my slavery to sin. I was no longer a slave to my ego, my pride, my lust, peer pressure, the desire to make money, or to please this evil world. I was set free from the power of sin and the grip of death. And through faith in Jesus I was able to deal with the fear of death that had haunted me all my life. It was as though I stood helpless and hopeless on the edge of a plane 10,000 feet up, knowing that I was about to jump, *when someone handed me a parachute that I knew would open*. Now I could control my fears. My fear would be in direct proportion to the faith I had in the parachute. Now, instead of plummeting to the ground at 120 mph to my death, I would float down at 8 mph to safety.

THROUGH FAITH IN JESUS I WAS ABLE TO DEAL WITH THE FEAR OF DEATH THAT HAD HAUNTED ME ALL MY LIFE.

When death ("the king of terrors," Job 18:14) comes for the Christian, it comes without a crown. It comes dethroned.

It is a lion without teeth. Death has no sting nor the grave any victory. The enemy has been defeated by the King of kings, and His brazen foot stands on the neck of the serpent.

A DIVINE APPOINTMENT

We each have a unique testimony, but in our salvation, we all have one thing in common. God draws sinners to Himself. Moses may have made a decision where to take the flock that day he was tending it, but we know better. He had an appointment with the God of his fathers. His Creator had designs for this lowly shepherd. He was going to shepherd God's people out of the bondage of Egypt.

Moses was attracted to the light of the fire because something didn't make sense. This was a bush that burned, but the branches weren't consumed by the flames.

To the world, the cross of Christ doesn't make sense; it is irrelevant. Millions see it as a mere symbol of the forgiveness of Jesus of Nazareth. Here was a Man who had been terribly wronged and yet He exercised the virtue of forgiveness from the very cross upon which He was impaled. His life and death are merely seen as an example for us to follow. These dear people are so close to knowing the truth, and yet they are strangers to salvation as long as they are not humbled by the moral Law. The purpose of the Ten Commandments is to show us that we can't earn everlasting life—that we are helpless and hopeless as guilty sinners.

To know that we can't save ourselves is humbling. Think of an Olympic swimmer. Everyone admires him because he's such a great swimmer. But one day he is caught in an ocean current that begins to pull him underwater. It's humbling for such an athlete to have to call for help, but he will do so *if he sees his life is in danger*.

The Law of Moses shows us that our life is in danger. Suddenly Jesus is seen as the ultimate lifeguard.

Without knowledge of our terrifying predicament, the cross is irrelevant. I don't need mercy while I'm convinced that I'm a good person. The Law changes that and makes mercy make sense, and that's attractive for guilty sinners. Our God is a consuming fire (Hebrews 12:29), but in Christ we are not consumed by the fire of His wrath. Justice was satisfied through the blood of the cross. The debt to the moral Law that called for *our* blood was satisfied by *His* blood. This happened the moment Jesus whispered, "It is finished!" (John 19:30). These are arguably the greatest three words uttered in human history. The sound of a million church bells signifying that death had been nullified would fall short of doing justice to such glorious good news.

THE DEBT TO THE MORAL LAW THAT CALLED FOR *OUR* BLOOD WAS SATISFIED BY *HIS* BLOOD.

But three days later in that cold corpse in the tomb, when that first tiny heartbeat chimed, it rang infinitely louder than those million bells. God put His smile of acceptance upon the sacrifice of the Lamb and Jesus rose from the grave.

> So when the LORD saw that he turned aside to look, God called to him from the midst of the bush and said, "Moses, Moses!" And he said, "Here I am." (Exodus 3:4)

God gives the universal call to repentance to every human being. He commands all men everywhere to repent (see Acts 17:30,31). Those who turn aside from this world to look intently at the cross will hear the voice of God calling him.

He knows each of us by name (John 10:3). He formed us in the womb and is the lover of our soul! Oh I thank God for the night that He drew me to Himself, called my name and enabled me to say, "Here I am."

But now my heart breaks when sinners refuse His call in Christ. There are no words to express the horror, the tragedy, the foolishness of a proud and rebellious sinner refusing mercy who will consequently reap wrath. He is welcoming death, pain, and suffering for eternity, and rejecting pleasure forevermore.

Let's still our hearts with a holy reverence as Almighty God then speaks to Moses:

> Then He said, "Do not draw near this place. Take your sandals off your feet, for the place where you stand is holy ground." Moreover He said, "I am the God of your father—the God of Abraham, the God of Isaac, and the God of Jacob." And Moses hid his face, for he was afraid to look upon God. (Exodus 3:5,6)

God merely manifested Himself in a burning bush. Then He told Moses not to approach Him, and even from where he stood he was to humble himself by removing his shoes, because he stood on holy ground. This was the God of Abraham, Isaac, and Jacob. And even with those instructions, and with that divine identification, Moses could not look upon God because fear filled his heart. These are the keys to a successful walk with our Creator. Moses greatly feared God and walked in humility of heart before Him.

Every day of our transient lives we must take off our shoes, so to speak, because we stand on holy ground. Each step we take in life we must take with a humble and God-fearing heart. That will ensure that we walk in obedience, and an obedient heart will ensure a life of victory over lust, pride, jealousy, greed, and our many other often besetting sins.

Now Moses was ready to hear why God had condescended to speak to one man:

> And the LORD said: "I have surely seen the oppression of My people who are in Egypt, and have heard their cry because of their taskmasters, for I know their sorrows. So I have come down to deliver them out of the hand of the Egyptians, and to bring them up from that land to a good and large land, to a land flowing with milk and honey, to the place of the Canaanites and the Hittites and the Amorites and the Perizzites and the Hivites and the Jebusites. Now therefore, behold, the cry of the children of Israel has come to Me, and I have also seen the oppression with which the Egyptians oppress them. Come now, therefore, and I will send you to Pharaoh that you may bring My people, the children of Israel, out of Egypt." (Exodus 3:7–10)

God has seen every sin-loving sinner. He knows them by name and knows every hair on every human head. Not a thought enters a heart or word flows from any tongue that He is not intimately familiar with (Psalm 139:1–3). He sees the oppression of the enemy who came to steal, kill, and destroy. Each slave of sin has the divine spark of eternity in his heart and cries to be free from death. Sin is the hardest of taskmasters because it pays the wages of death (Romans 6:23).

Almighty God commissioned this meek and lowly-of-heart shepherd to be His representative. He chose Moses to be His spokesperson to take the message of freedom to oppressed slaves.

But Moses said to God, "Who am I that I should go to Pharaoh, and that I should bring the children of Israel out of Egypt?" (Exodus 3:11)

WHO AM I?

Are we *honored* that God has commissioned us to preach the gospel to every creature? Jesus said, "Go into all the world and preach the gospel to every creature" (Mark 16:15). This command is to *every* Christian. If it was exclusive to the first twelve disciples, then the gospel would have died out when they died. So how do we respond to this honor? No doubt you are like me and have very real fears at the thought of speaking to the ungodly. We tremble and say, "Who am I that I should approach strangers with the gospel?"

But my attempt to wriggle out of the uncomfortable task of evangelism may come from a subtle and false humility. Sinners are going to Hell but who am I to warn them? I'm a nobody. Or I could be more honest and say that sinners are asleep while their house is on fire, *and I don't care*. Whatever the excuse, it is weak at best, cowardly at worst. Shame on me if I do nothing while another human being burns to death:

ARE WE *HONORED* THAT GOD HAS COMMISSIONED US TO PREACH THE GOSPEL TO EVERY CREATURE?

> But you, beloved, building yourselves up on your most holy faith, praying in the Holy Spirit, keep yourselves in the love of God, looking for the mercy of our Lord Jesus Christ unto eternal life. And on some have compassion, making a distinction; but others save with fear,

pulling them out of the fire, hating even the garment defiled by the flesh. (Jude 20–23)

If evangelism scares you, do what Scripture says and "build yourselves up on your most holy faith." Pray, and keep yourself in the love of God—because love is your motivation. Love will shake off fear, apathy, selfishness, and the false humility that is more worried about our own (so often unrealized) fears than the fact that dying sinners are going to Hell. We have obtained mercy, and as unprofitable servants we must run to do His will—especially in light of the love of the cross. Besides, as God was with Moses, so He will be with us. Look at His kind and patient words of assurance to Moses:

"I will certainly be with you. And this shall be a sign to you that I have sent you: When you have brought the people out of Egypt, you shall serve God on this mountain." (Exodus 3:12)

Jesus said that He would certainly be with us:

"All authority has been given to Me in heaven and on earth. Go therefore and make disciples of all the nations, baptizing them in the name of the Father and of the Son and of the Holy Spirit, teaching them to observe all things that I have commanded you; and lo, I am with you always, even to the end of the age." (Matthew 28:18–20)

What more could we want? We are not alone in this daunting task. Neither would Moses be alone, but look at his response:

Then Moses said to God, "Indeed, when I come to the children of Israel and say to them, 'The God of your fathers has sent me to you,' and they say to me, 'What is His name?' what shall I say to them?" (Exodus 3:13)

The first excuse Moses gave was "Who am I?" That didn't work, so he moved to "Who are You?" We too are not confined to one excuse. What if sinners ask a question I can't answer? What if they ask me for evidence that God exists, or why God allows suffering, or why there are so many hypocrites in the church? Or what if they say, "Who are you to speak for God?" What do I say?

All these questions may seem hard to answer, but most have easy explanations. Besides, when we learn the principles of biblical evangelism (covered later in the book) they become almost irrelevant. If you rush into a burning two-story apartment and awaken its sleeping residents to a fire in the first floor, they may have legitimate questions. They may ask who you are and who sent you. They may want to know if you have called the fire department, and they may wonder how long it will be until they arrive. But these questions will be set aside because of their immediate and terrible danger. If they smell the smoke and see the flames, the questions, legitimate though they may be, aren't of immediate importance. What is important is that they run from the building and get out of danger.

Consider the apostle Paul's motivation to warn every person:

To them God willed to make known what are the riches of the glory of this mystery among the Gentiles: which is Christ in you, the hope of glory. Him we preach, warning every man and teaching every man in all wisdom, that we may present every man perfect in Christ Jesus. (Colossians 1:27–28)

We have Christ in us, the hope of glory! We are sealed with the source of life itself. There is no greater treasure on this earth. All the gold, diamonds, and pearls stacked as a massive mountain are but stinking trash compared to what we have in Christ. He is our hope of glory. And it's Him we preach, suffering on a cross for the sin of the world, rising from the dead and defeating death! We do this because they must be warned. *Everyone* must be warned. They are in terrible danger, and they will be damned unless they are made perfect in Christ Jesus.

Then notice what Paul says:

> To this end I also labor, striving according to His working which works in me mightily. (Colossians 1:29)

As God was with Moses, He was with Paul, and He is with us *always*. Our job as Christians is to bear witness of the truth, and the way to do that is to do what Jesus did in so many places. Open up the Law of Moses and let them see that they have failed to keep it. Let them smell the smoke of God's indignation and see the flames of His coming wrath against their sin. Fear is the factor that will get those who are asleep to run out of a burning building, and fear will cause sinners to flee from God's wrath:

> And by the fear of the LORD one departs from evil. (Proverbs 16:6)

Only a fool would want to stay in a burning building, and blind sinners will remain in sin until a healthy fear begins to dawn on their darkened understanding. The moral Law shows them the insanity of staying in sin. They have been asleep in the bed of iniquity, but the Commandments awaken them. Never downplay or despise fear in your evangelistic message. Without it sinners will stay in their sins and end up in Hell. Look at what Jesus said about it:

> "For there is nothing covered that will not be revealed, nor hidden that will not be known. Therefore whatever you have spoken in the dark will be heard in the light, and what you have spoken in the ear in inner rooms will be proclaimed on the housetops.
>
> "And I say to you, My friends, do not be afraid of those who kill the body, and after that have no more that they can do. But I will show you whom you should fear: Fear Him who, after He has killed, has power to cast into hell; yes, I say to you, fear Him!" (Luke 12:2–5)

God is to be feared because of His power, because He has appointed a day on which He will judge the world in righteousness, and because a terrible place called Hell awaits those who have transgressed His Law. It is a fearful thing to fall into the hands of the living God (Hebrews 10:31). The questions about suffering, or hypocrites in the church, or who are you to be representing God, etc., are usually asked because the sinner is skeptical about you or your message.

WE HAVE CHRIST IN US, THE HOPE OF GLORY! WE ARE SEALED WITH THE SOURCE OF LIFE ITSELF.

But when a sinner smells the smoke and sees the flames, it will suddenly dawn on him that you *do* care for him. He understands that attempts to awaken him are motivated by love and kindness. When he sees that he is in terrible danger, his questions become secondary to the issue at hand—his eternal salvation.

THE QUESTION OF WHO SENT MOSES

The concern that Moses had, that those in Egypt would ask who it was that had sent him, may have been legitimate. It may not have just been an excuse that he was giving to try to avoid the task. He was asked that question forty years earlier as he tried to break up a fight between two Hebrew men: *"Who made you a prince and a judge over us?* Do you intend to kill me as you killed the Egyptian?"* (Exodus 2:13,14).

That traumatic moment had burned into his memory. Perhaps he had a fear that the haunting question would come back to him if he returned to Egypt: *Who made you a prince and a judge over us?* It was a curveball, and he had no comeback. Stephen's farewell speech eloquently fills in the details of that event:

> Now when he was forty years old, it came into his heart to visit his brethren, the children of Israel. And seeing one of them suffer wrong, he defended and avenged him who was oppressed, and struck down the Egyptian. For he supposed that his brethren would have understood that God would deliver them by his hand, but they did not understand. And the next day he appeared to two of them as they were fighting, and tried to reconcile them, saying, "Men, you are brethren; why do you wrong one another?" But he who did his neighbor wrong pushed him away, saying, "Who made you a ruler and a judge over us? Do you want to kill me as you did the Egyptian yesterday?" (Acts 7:23–28)

Moses thought they would understand that God would deliver them by his hand. But they didn't understand. "Who made you a ruler and a judge over us?" was asked then as a rhetorical question. Now it had a wonderful answer:

44

And God said to Moses, "I AM WHO I AM." And He said, "Thus you shall say to the children of Israel, 'I AM has sent me to you.'" (Exodus 3:14)

The website GotQuestions.org gives us more insight into the significance of this phrase:

The phrase translated "I am who I am" in Hebrew is *ehyeh asher ehyeh*. The word *ehyeh* is the first person common singular of the verb *to be*. It would be used in any number of normal situations: "I am watching the sheep," "I am walking on the road," or "I am his father." However, when used as a stand-alone description, *I AM* is the ultimate statement of self-sufficiency, self-existence, and immediate presence. God's existence is not contingent upon anyone else. His plans are not contingent upon any circumstances. He promises that He will be what He will be; that is, He will be the eternally constant God. He stands, ever-present and unchangeable, completely sufficient in Himself to do what He wills to do and to accomplish what He wills to accomplish.[3]

When it comes to sharing God's message, you too may have legitimate fears because of some haunting memory. I do. I relate in detail in my life story (*Out of the Comfort Zone*) how I was humiliated beyond words as a sixteen-year-old student. I was terrified of public speaking, and found myself on a list to give speeches in my English class. The thought of standing up in front of my peers was so frightening, I stayed away from school during that Tuesday class. But I couldn't get out of it when eventually my name was the only one left on the list. I stood up to talk for a few minutes about my passion—surfing. I thought I could manage that. But halfway through the speech my fear suddenly swallowed me and my mind went blank. *Really* blank. It was a slow-motion nightmare that more than forty years later still has the power to take my breath away and even bring tears to my eyes if I let it. I humiliated myself in front of my peers, and that's a huge deal when you are sixteen. It was my deadly "deer in the headlights" moment. I didn't recover as I stood there—I died a thousand deaths. All I could do was slink back to my seat in humiliation.

But when I came to the Savior, I was immediately aware that I AM had commissioned me and every other Christian to warn sinners that they are in terrible danger. That brought my fears into perspective. What sort of hardhearted cowardly jerk would I be to let sinners go to Hell because I had some distant memory that sealed my selfish lips? Shame on me if I didn't warn them:

> For if I preach the gospel, I have nothing to boast of, for necessity is laid upon me; yes, woe is me if I do not preach the gospel! (1 Corinthians 9:16)

If the world asks who sent you, tell them that I AM did, *but be careful how you word your answer.* Mental institutions are filled with people who think that they are Jesus, or that they are messengers from God, or that they hear voices telling them to kill people. To say that I AM told you to speak to unbelievers may put you in that category of craziness. So always quickly qualify the answer by saying that every Christian is a missionary who has been divinely commissioned to tell the world that God has destroyed their greatest enemy. Death has been overcome by the power of the gospel.

One way to explain the gospel is to tell the unsaved that the message of the Bible is simple. *The Old Testament was God's promise that He would destroy death, and the New Tes-*

tament tells us how He did it. To the unsaved, the Scriptures are a dry history book, and to have it summarized in such a way *with that claim* is both fresh and unique. Who in his right mind wouldn't at least perk up an ear at the thought? Simplistic though it may sound, that's the message of the Bible. In the Old Testament God pulled back the bow. In Christ He fired the arrow... and the target was our greatest enemy. How can we not be consumed with reaching dying sinners with such good news? Look at how the Bible speaks of this, and of the consequent conclusion (the "therefore"):

> "O Death, where is your sting?
> O Hades, where is your victory?"

> The sting of death is sin, and the strength of sin is the law. But thanks be to God, who gives us the victory through our Lord Jesus Christ. *Therefore*, my beloved brethren, be steadfast, immovable, always abounding in the work of the Lord, knowing that your labor is not in vain in the Lord. (1 Corinthians 15:55–58)

There is a way to make this difficult task much easier. We will look at that in the next chapter.

CHAPTER Four

OUR AGENDA

It took me years of trial and error, but I finally came up with a unique and inoffensive way to bring up the subject of the gospel with strangers—using appealing gospel tracts as icebreakers.

I was sitting in a hospital waiting room with three other people. Two were about 30 feet to my left, and about 15 feet to my right was a lady in her mid thirties who was messing around with her phone. So how do I share the gospel with someone in that sort of environment? One approach I have been using lately is to hand out a business card-sized tract with a cute picture of my dog, Sam, and me riding a bicycle. The wind was causing his long ears to flow back, and he was obviously lapping up the experience. Across the bottom of the colorful card were the bold words "YouTube. Over 80,000,000 views: Living Waters."

I stood up and walked toward her, saying, "Excuse me. Do you like dogs?" She immediately looked up from her phone and responded with an enthusiastic, "Yes." I held out the card and said, "This is my dog. He's wearing sunglasses." She reacted with a broad smile and the usual, "How cute!" I handed her the card and said, "I have a YouTube channel with over 80 million views. I ask people if they think there's an afterlife. Do *you* think there's an afterlife?"

Another approach is to use a gospel tract, such as our popular Million Dollar Bill, which people are always delighted to receive. It looks just like a real million (if there was such a thing) and has the million-dollar question on the back: "Will you go to Heaven when you die?" You could then simply ask, "Do you think there's an afterlife?"

When she said that she believed there was, I asked, "Do you think about it much?" She said that she did, and this is how the conversation went from there.

"What is your name?"

"Angelina."

"Angelina, do you think you'll make it to Heaven? Are you a good person?"

Most people have no idea of what God requires of them. They intuitively know that He requires morality—that they need to be good—but they don't know the extent of that goodness. Biblically, it means to be morally perfect. Asking the question, "Do you think you're a good person?" gives you opportunity to explain His standard.

She said that she was, so it was time for Moses to prepare her for Jesus. I replied, "How many lies do you think you've told in your whole life?"

"Lots."

"Have you ever stolen something?"

"Yes."

"Have you ever used God's name in vain?"

"Yes, I have."

"Jesus said that if you look with lust you commit adultery in your heart. Have you ever looked with lust?"

"Yes. In my teenage years."

50

"Angelina, I'm not judging you, but you have just told me that you are a lying thief, a blasphemer, and an adulterer at heart. If God judges you by the Ten Commandments on Judgment Day (we have looked at four), are you going to be innocent or guilty?"

"Guilty."

"Heaven or Hell?"

"Hell."

"Does that concern you?"

The Puritans would speak of a sinner being "awakened" and being "alarmed." *Awakened* would be to understand that the parachute you are wearing isn't going to open. *Alarmed* is when you recognize your mortal danger. An awakened sinner needs to hear more Law, and God's wrath against lawbreakers, to move him from knowing that Hell exists to being horrified that he's going there. That concern will help him to understand the gospel. He will only flee to the cross when he sees he's in big trouble. If he doesn't have concern, he will stay in his sins.

"Yes," she replied.

The Law had done its wonderful work. It had prepared her heart for grace. To use another analogy, no one is going to appreciate a cure if they don't first admit they have a disease. The moral Law diagnoses the disease of sin, and the gospel is the divine prescription. When I then shared the cross with Angelina, and the necessity for her to repent and trust in Jesus alone, she was very receptive and very thankful.

When I asked her why she was in the waiting room, she said her father had just died of an aneurysm and the doctors thought it was genetic. She was there for tests, and she was no doubt afraid and very prayerful. Perhaps this short encounter had been divinely orchestrated. I trusted that it had.

As I was called away for my appointment, Angelina said that she would definitely check out the YouTube channel.

BACK TO THE BURNING BUSH

I AM had personally commissioned Moses and addressed his fear that if he returned to Egypt those who once asked who made him a deliverer would ask who it was that sent him. Moses was to tell them that I AM, the God of Abraham, Isaac, and Jacob, had sent him. But fear was deeply ingrained into Moses. Even in the face of Almighty God Himself assuring him that He would go with him, Moses argued,

"But suppose they will not believe me or listen to my voice; suppose they say, 'The LORD has not appeared to you.'" (Exodus 4:1)

What if sinners don't believe me? What if no one listens to me? What if they think I'm delusional, or my mind goes blank? But fears are not from within. They are not of our own making. If we had our way we would run to do God's will without a second thought. These negative thoughts that seek to paralyze us are from without. We have an enemy that has a barrage of fiery "*What if*" darts aimed at you and me to discourage us from the Great Commission.

Here's how to do battle:

Above all, taking the shield of faith with which you will be able to quench all the fiery darts of the wicked one. (Ephesians 6:16)

The shield of our trust in God stops those arrows from penetrating our hearts. We trust God no matter what. So what if they don't believe? We can't make them believe us. If they refuse to, that's between them and God. It doesn't matter if they won't listen or if they mock us. What matters is that I'm faithful to my commission. However, I find that almost all my fears are unfounded. Sinners do believe. They do listen, and when the gospel is presented lovingly and biblically, they realize that they are the ones who are deceived by sin. Look at Scripture telling us to be strong in the Lord. That's an attitude we are to embrace:

> Finally, my brethren, be strong in the Lord and in the power of His might. Put on the whole armor of God, that you may be able to stand against the wiles of the devil. For we do not wrestle against flesh and blood, but against principalities, against powers, against the rulers of the darkness of this age, against spiritual hosts of wickedness in the heavenly places. Therefore take up the whole armor of God, that you may be able to withstand in the evil day, and having done all, to stand. (Ephesians 6:10–13)

One day I approached about a dozen of what looked like members of a gang. Most of them were covered in tattoos. I said my usual, "Hey, guys. Anyone like to do an interview on YouTube? My channel has over eighty million views." A number of them immediately said they were in. I smiled and said, "You don't even know what it's about. I ask people if they think there's an afterlife. What do you think?" One said there definitely was, another said there wasn't.

Over the next thirty minutes I shared the gospel with three very colorful characters. No one got angry. No one was killed. Instead, three hardened human beings heard the how to have eternal life, and everyone got five-dollar gift cards. And I came away from that witnessing encounter clicking my little heels.

Let your conscience remind you to get up off the couch of complacency and ignore your fears. It's going to take effort to get up and go. I have to daily fight apathy, laziness, doubt, selfishness, fear, and a bombardment of disgusting thoughts. These fiery darts are never-ending, but I'm always aware that God will be with me when I get up and go.

Let me now address something I mentioned earlier. I said, "It was time for Moses to prepare her for Jesus." When Moses told the LORD that his hearers may not believe what he said, we read something wonderful:

> So the LORD said to him, "What is that in your hand?"
> He said, "A rod."
> And He said, "Cast it on the ground." So he cast it on the ground, and it became a serpent; and Moses fled from it. Then the LORD said to Moses, "Reach out your hand and take it by the tail" (and he reached out his hand and caught it, and it became a rod in his hand), "that they may believe that the LORD God of their fathers, the God of Abraham, the God of Isaac, and the God of Jacob, has appeared to you." (Exodus 4:2–5)

Back in 1982, by the grace of God, I discovered that God had put the rod of Moses into my hand. At the time I was extremely frustrated that my evangelism was fruitless. Sinners didn't believe me when shared the gospel. It was like water off a sinful duck's greasy back. But on one memorable Friday afternoon I read a portion of a Charles Spurgeon sermon with widened eyes. He was using the Law of Moses when he spoke to sinners.

Here is a portion of his sermon:

> What will you do when the law comes in terror, when the trumpet of the archangel shall tear you from your

grave, when the eyes of God shall burn their way into your guilty soul, when the great books shall be opened, and all your sin and shame shall be punished? Can you stand against an angry law in that day?[4]

I wondered what the great preacher was doing and tucked it into my memory banks. Two days later I read Galatians 3:24:

Therefore the law was our tutor to bring us to Christ, that we might be justified by faith.

I had always read it as the Law being a tutor to bring *Israel* to Christ. It was like a light switched on in my head. I ran out and experimented on a sinner, and found to my delight that the Law did bring the knowledge of sin, just as Scripture says:

Now we know that whatever the law says, it says to those who are under the law, that every mouth may be stopped, and all the world may become guilty before God. Therefore by the deeds of the law no flesh will be justified in His sight, for by the law is the knowledge of sin. (Romans 3:19,20)

Each of us have that same rod of Moses in our hand and we can "cast it on the ground." When we lay the moral Law before a guilty sinner, it becomes a biting serpent. Paul said that the Law (the Commandment) brought death to him (see Romans 7:13). Jesus used this illustration when He spoke of the gospel:

"And as Moses lifted up the serpent in the wilderness, even so must the Son of Man be lifted up, that whoever believes in Him should not perish but have eternal life.

For God so loved the world that He gave His only be-gotten Son, that whoever believes in Him should not perish but have everlasting life." (John 3:14–16)

When we open up the moral Law as Jesus did (see Mark 10:17,18, and in the Sermon on the Mount), those congenial Commandments suddenly turn on sinners, and their bite is fatal. It dawns on them that the Law doesn't save; it kills. It calls for our death sentence and steers us toward our only means of escape. The gospel is the sinful soul's sole solution. It is the only antidote. When that revelation comes, faith comes with it, in that the gospel becomes credible. The rod does its God-given work "that they may believe that the LORD God of their fathers, the God of Abraham, the God of Isaac, and the God of Jacob, has appeared to you."

THE GOSPEL IS THE SINFUL SOUL'S SOLE SOLUTION. IT IS THE ONLY ANTIDOTE.

Consider this rather lengthy, but wonderful quote from Charles Spurgeon about the rightful use of the Law:

The objection supposed may be worded thus: "You say, O Paul, that the law cannot justify; surely then the law is good for nothing at all; 'Wherefore then serveth the law?' If it will not save a man, what is the good of it? If of itself it will never take a man to heaven, why was it written? Is it not a useless thing?"

The apostle might have replied to his opponent with a sneer—he must have said to him, "Oh, fool, and slow of heart to understand. Is it proved that a thing is utterly useless because it is not intended for every pur-pose in the world? Will you say that, because iron cannot be eaten, therefore, iron is not useful? And because gold cannot be the food of man, will you, therefore, cast gold away, and call it worthless dross? Yet on your foolish supposition you must do so. For, because I have said the law cannot save, you have foolishly asked me what is the use of it? and you foolishly suppose God's law is good for nothing, and can be of no value whatever."

This objection is, generally, brought forward by two sorts of people. First, by mere cavillers who do not like the gospel, and wish to pick all sorts of holes in it. They can tell us what they do not believe; but they do not tell us what they do believe. They would fight with everybody's doctrines and sentiments, but they would be at a loss if they were asked to sit down and write their own opinions. They do not seem to have got much further than the genius of the monkey, which can pull everything to pieces, but can put nothing together.

Then, on the other hand, there is the Antinomian, who says, "Yes, I know I am saved by grace alone;" and then breaks the law—says, it is not binding on him, even as a rule of life; and asks, "Wherefore then serveth the law?" throwing it out of his door as an old piece of furniture only fit for the fire, because, forsooth, it is not adapted to save his soul. Why, a thing may have many uses, if not a particular one. It is true that the law cannot save; and yet it is equally true that the law is one of the highest works of God, and is deserving of all reverence, and extremely useful when applied by God to the purposes for which it was intended.

Yet, pardon me my friends, if I just observe that this is a very natural question, too. If you read the doctrine of the apostle Paul you find him declaring that the law condemns all mankind. Now, just let us for one single moment take a bird's eye view of the works of the law in this world. Lo, I see, the law given upon Mount Sinai. The very hill doth quake with fear. Lightnings and thunders are the attendants of those dreadful syllables which make the hearts of Israel to melt. Sinai seemeth altogether on the smoke. The Lord came from Paran, and the Holy One from Mount Sinai; "He came with ten thousand of his saints." Out of his mouth went a fiery law for them. It was a dread law even when it was given, and since then from that Mount of Sinai an awful lava of vengeance has run down, to deluge, to destroy, to burn, and to consume the whole human race, if it had not been that Jesus Christ had stemmed its awful torrent, and bidden its waves of fire be still.

If you could see the world without Christ in it, simply under the law you would see a world in ruins, a world with God's black seal put upon it, stamped and sealed for condemnation; you would see men, who, if they knew their condition, would have their hands on their loins and be groaning all their days—you would see men and women condemned, lost, and ruined; and in the uttermost regions you would see the pit that is digged for the wicked, into which the whole earth must have been cast if the law had its way, apart from the gospel of Jesus Christ our Redeemer.

Ay, beloved, the law is a great deluge which would have drowned the world with worse than the water of Noah's flood, it is a great fire which would have burned the earth with a destruction worse than that which fell on Sodom, it is a stern angel with a sword, athirst for blood, and winged to slay; it is a great destroyer sweeping down the nations; it is the great messenger of God's vengeance sent into the world. Apart from the gospel of

Jesus Christ, the law is nothing but the condemning voice of God thundering against mankind. "Wherefore then serveth the law?" seems a very natural question. Can the law be of any benefit to man? Can that Judge who puts on a black cap and condemns us all, this Lord Chief Justice Law, can he help in salvation? Yes, he did; and you shall see how he does it, if God shall help us while we preach. "Wherefore then serveth the law?"

The first use of the law is *to manifest to man his guilt*. When God intends to save a man, the first thing he does with him is to send the law to him, to show him how guilty, how vile, how ruined he is, and in how dangerous a position.[5]

LEGITIMATE QUESTIONS

Often, I've had a great discussion with someone to a point where they've moved from being an atheist to becoming a theist. They suddenly believe in God. They have heard the Law and they see their danger. Many times I've had people say, "I have enjoyed this, but I have some questions. Maybe you could help me."

Perhaps that thought makes you a little nervous, because you don't see yourself as an apologist. But you need not have an answer for every question. If I don't have an answer, I say so. But if we do have an answer, it could be beneficial in helping someone come to the cross.

What if someone asks if homosexuality is a sin? We don't want to compromise God's Word, but we also don't want to be accused of being "homophobic." Especially when we don't hate anyone. We are not fornicatorphobic, nor liarphobic, nor are we thiefphobic. We love everyone enough to warn them that God is just and that He commands everyone to turn from all sin if they want to live. Love will speak the truth, in love.

During a three-hour lull in a rainstorm that lasted for four days in Southern California, I ventured out to look for people to share the gospel with. After about twenty minutes of asking different people, I found one gentleman who was very congenial to the things of God.

His name was JoJo. He thought Heaven and Hell did exist and that he would go to Heaven because he was a good person. I shared the gospel with him by first taking him through the Ten Commandments. He said that he had told many lies. He had also stolen and had blasphemed God's name, adding, "I try not to."

Then I told him, "Jesus said, 'Whoever looks upon a woman to lust for her has committed adultery already with her and his heart.'" He looked at me and said, "I haven't done that, but I have lusted after men." I asked, "Are you homosexual?" to which he predictably replied that he was.

Here is the wonderful thing about the Law of Moses. The Bible tells us that it was made for sinners, and it lists homosexuals among them:

> Now we know [without any doubt] that the Law is good, if one uses it lawfully and appropriately, understanding the fact that law is not enacted for the righteous person [the one in right standing with God], but for lawless and rebellious people, for the ungodly and sinful, for the irreverent and profane, for those who kill their fathers or mothers, for murderers, for sexually immoral persons, *for homosexuals*, for kidnappers and slave traders, for liars, for perjurers—and for whatever else is contrary to sound doctrine, according to the glo-

rious gospel of the blessed God, with which I have been entrusted. (1 Timothy 1:8–11, AMP)

Instead of telling him that his homosexual lifestyle was a sin in the sight of God, I deliberately ignored the issue. I wanted to share the gospel with him without shutting down the conversation because of a lack of discretion, and I could do this because the Law was made for homosexuals.

JoJo needed to see that he was in terrible danger. And that would cause him to listen to the gospel with a humble heart (see Romans 3:19,20). After we had looked at some of the Commandments, I said, "JoJo, I'm not judging you, but you've just told me that you are a lying, thieving, blasphemous adulterer at heart. And you have to face God on Judgment Day." When he told me that these things were done in the past, I said that if he were in court and told the judge that his crimes were "in the past," the judge would probably be incredulous, because everything but the future is in the past. We can't hold on to the present for a millisecond.

I said that he would be guilty on Judgment Day and would end up in Hell. I told him, "JoJo, the Bible says that all liars will be cast into the lake of fire, that no thief, no blasphemer, no adulterer would enter the Kingdom of God." Then I asked, "What can you do to escape the damnation of Hell?" saying that that was the most important question he would ever be asked.

He didn't know. So I shared the good news that Jesus paid the penalty for our sin on the cross. That meant that God could dismiss our case and grant us everlasting life as a gift—all because of the death and resurrection of Jesus Christ. Then I said to a humble JoJo, "What you have to do is repent and trust in Jesus alone. That means that you turn from *all* of your sins—lying, stealing, blasphemy, adultery, fornication, *and homosexuality*, which the Bible says is a sin in the sight of God. If you don't repent of all sin, it means that you will be playing the hypocrite and end up in Hell."

JoJo wasn't offended. He listened with an open heart. The Law had done its wonderful work. There wasn't even a hint of an accusation of hate-speech in his eyes. Thanks to the *reasonableness* of condemnation by the moral Law, he could see that my motive was one of love and concern. Without the God-given rod of Moses to cast down at his sinful feet, what I would have said about his sexuality would have almost certainly either been mocked, been ignored, or stirred his anger.

THOUGH OUR SINS WERE AS SCARLET, THEY ARE WHITE AS SNOW BECAUSE OF GOD'S GREAT MERCY.

I then gave him a booklet called "Save Yourself Some Pain" and thanked him for listening to me. He was very grateful, we said our goodbyes, and I left, praying for this lost sinner and thanking God that he had listened.

ANOTHER WEAPON

We have another powerful weapon in the battle to reach the lost. In Exodus 4:6–8 we read that God told Moses to put his hand into his bosom, and when he removed it, his hand was leprous, like snow. Then the LORD told him to put his hand in again and when he drew it out of his bosom, it was restored like his other flesh. And God then said, "Then it will be, if they do not believe you, nor heed the message of the first sign, that they may believe the message of the latter sign" (v. 8).

Those who know the Lord have the testimony that our hearts were once filled with sin, but we have been cleansed and forgiven. Though our sins were as scarlet, they are white as snow because of God's great mercy.

Spurgeon speaks of the contrite sinner, who sees his wicked heart, being cleansed by the grace of God:

> He stands before us, and with many a sigh and tear, confesses that he is utterly ruined and undone. "Sir, a month or two ago I would have claimed a righteousness with the very best of them. I, too, could have boasted of what I have done; but now I see my righteousness to be as filthy rags, and all my goodness is as an unclean thing. I count all these things but dross and dung. I tread upon them and despise them. I have done no good thing. I have sinned and come short of the glory of God. If ever there was a sinner that deserved to be damned, sir, that soul am I; if ever there was one who had not any excuse to make, but who must plead guilty, without any extenuating circumstances, that man am I.
>
> As for the future, I can make no promise, I have often promised, and so often lied. I have so often trusted in myself that I would reform, so often have I hoped the energy of my nature might yet heal my disease, that I renounce, because I cannot help renouncing all such desires.
>
> "Lord, if ever I am made whole, thy grace must make me so. I do desire to be rid of sin; but I can no more rid myself of sin than I can pluck the sun from the firmament, or scoop the waters from the depth of the sea. I would be perfect, even as thou art perfect; but I cannot change my heart. As well might the viper lose his will to poison, the Ethiopian change his skin, or the

leopard his spots, as I cease to do evil. Lord, at thy feet I fall, full of leprosy from head to foot; nothing have I to boast of, nothing to trust to except thy mercy."

My brother, you are a clean leper; your sins are forgiven you, your iniquities are put away. Through the blood of Jesus Christ, who died upon the tree, you are saved. As soon as ever the leprosy had come right out, the man was clean, and as soon as ever your sin is fully manifest, so that in your conscience you feel yourself to be really a sinner, there is a way of salvation for you. Then by the sprinkling of blood and the washing of water, you may be made clean.[6]

Our personal testimony is a witness to the truth of the gospel. We were full of sin but are now new creatures in Christ. This is what I tell those who hear the Law and still try to justify themselves. If they believed, they would see their danger, humble themselves, and flee from wrath. But their excuses about telling only "white" lies, or stealing only small things, and saying that *everyone* lusts reveals that they don't see sin as being serious. I therefore emphasize my testimony and say that I once loved darkness and hated the light, but God cleansed me and granted me everlasting life through my faith in Jesus.

And if the person hears the Law, hears my testimony, and is still hardhearted, there is one more powerful truth we can give them:

> "And it shall be, if they do not believe even these two signs, or listen to your voice, that you shall take water from the river and pour it on the dry land. The water which you take from the river will become blood on the dry land." (Exodus 4:9)

When unsaved people hear the gospel and still refuse mercy, we have to pour on wrath. We have to go back to the Law and say that God means what He says about sin. He is *deadly* serious, and He will damn all who give themselves to evil. I often look hardhearted sinners in the eye and say with a loving and concerned tone, "If your eyes meet my eyes on Judgment Day and you're still in your sins, I'm free from your blood because I've told you the truth. On that Day you will cry out, *"Why didn't you slap my face to awaken me?!"* But if I did that it would offend you. All I can do is slap you with words, which I'm doing because I love you." I further explain that "death" is wages that God pays to those who serve sin:

For the wages of sin is death... (Romans 6:23)

A judge sentences a murderer to death because he deserves it; he *earned* that sentence. It was due to him. And we all *earn* death. It is due to us as a payment because we served sin by our lies, theft, lust, blasphemy, etc. And while we speak to sinners and pour on the judgment and wrath of God, we have tears in our eyes and voice, praying that our hearers will come to their senses as they sit in the pigsty of sin.

Even though God has given us these powerfully effective weapons of warfare, most of us still struggle with the burdensome task of evangelism, and we will do anything we can to get out of any involvement.

Listen to Moses try yet again to wriggle out of it:

"O my Lord, I am not eloquent, neither before nor since You have spoken to Your servant; but I am slow of speech and slow of tongue." (Exodus 4:10)

It seems like Moses was saying that he didn't know what to say, that he found relating to people to be difficult. He lacked the necessary quick wit for what he was being asked to do. God's reply was to assure Moses again that He would be with him and would teach him what to say (v. 12). As he stepped out in faith, he would have divine training wheels.

Moses then suggested God send someone else. *Anyone* else, as long as it wasn't him. Finally, God's patience ran out, His anger was stirred, and He said that Aaron would come alongside Moses and be his helper.

Dear fellow trembler and excuse-maker, we have been given a greater helper than Aaron. God has given us His Holy Spirit as our helper:

> "And I will pray the Father, and He will give you another Helper, that He may abide with you forever." (John 14:16)

It is through Him that we have the power to be witnesses:

> But you shall receive power when the Holy Spirit has come upon you; and you shall be witnesses to Me in Jerusalem, and in all Judea and Samaria, and to the end of the earth. (Acts 1:8)

The apostle Paul also shoots down our excuses about not having quick wit and eloquence:

> And I, brethren, when I came to you, did not come with excellence of speech or of wisdom declaring to you the testimony of God. For I determined not to know anything among you except Jesus Christ and Him crucified. I was with you in weakness, in fear, and in much trembling. And my speech and my preaching were not with persuasive words of human wisdom, but in demonstration of the Spirit and of power, that your faith should not be in the wisdom of men but in the power of God. (1 Corinthians 2:1–5)

If you are a believer, the Holy Spirit dwells in you. You don't need anything else. You don't need to worry about a lack of eloquence, a lack of quick wit, or a lack of persuasive ability. All we need to worry about is a lack of obedience to what we have been commanded to do.

FOUR IMPORTANT TRUTHS

Let me comfort you for a moment in your excuses. Our sobering agenda is to bring sinners to the Savior, and granted, we do have a problem. The world loves the darkness and hates the light (John 3:19). How then can we possibly bring them to the light when they hate it? They don't want to come. They aren't even slightly interested. The odds are that they will be irritated by us, and so we feel like annoying telemarketers or door-to-door salesmen. We know that we would close the door or hang up the phone if we were in their position.

But we have something that *will* get their ear—if we can get them to lend it to us for a moment. *We have found everlasting life.* We know that fact, and they don't.

We also know these four truths:

1. Sinners have a God-given will to live. No one in their right mind wants to die.

2. They have an inherent knowledge of God. This is God-given, as Romans 1:18–20 makes clear. That knowledge is so obvious that it leaves them without excuse.

3. They also have a God-given conscience (Romans 2:15). It is an independent voice that echoes the truth of the moral Law. They cannot, in good conscience, deny the sinfulness of lying, stealing, murder, adultery, idolatry, parental dishonor, and blasphemy. These are prevalent human

sins named by Jesus and listed in other portions of Scripture.

4. Sinners are preprogrammed by God to respond to love, as we saw happen with JoJo.

The correct use of the Law covers all four of these truths. Its purpose is to bring the knowledge of sin and to show that sin is "exceedingly sinful" in God's sight (see Romans 7:7,13), and *that* knowledge shows the sinner that he's in danger of damnation in Hell. This was what Paul was doing in Romans chapter 2, when he picked up the biting serpent by its tail:

> You who preach that a man should not steal, do you steal? You who say, "Do not commit adultery," do you commit adultery? You who abhor idols, do you rob temples? You who make your boast in the law, do you dishonor God through breaking the law? For "the name of God is blasphemed among the Gentiles because of you," as it is written. (Romans 2:21–24)

This right use of the moral Law stirs a seared conscience so that it does its duty:

> ...for when Gentiles, who do not have the law, by nature do the things in the law, these, although not having the law, are a law to themselves, who show the work of the law written in their hearts, their conscience also bearing witness, and between themselves their thoughts accusing or else excusing them. (Romans 2:14,15)

As the conscience awakens and sin is seen as being deadly, the serpent strikes—and wrath becomes reasonable as the sinner sees his terrible danger. Suddenly you're not viewed as an obnoxious salesman or annoying telemarketer, but as a heroic firefighter who is trying to save his precious life. He sees that you are warning him *because you love him.*

We must never hold back hard biblical truths because we fear rejection, and if we can uncompromisingly present them and keep them palatable, we do well. And knowing that we can do this will reduce our fears.

Listen to Charles Spurgeon address our temptation to be intimidated by fear:

THIS RIGHT USE OF THE MORAL LAW STIRS A SEARED CONSCIENCE SO THAT IT DOES ITS DUTY.

"My brother in the gospel, what if you and I should keep back some painful part of God's message, and God should do so to us, and more also? I cannot bear to be lost; and yet I shall be lost if I decline to warn others of their danger, and of the doom of unbelief. I cannot bear to be cast away for ever from the presence of God; yet this woe will be unto me if I preach not the gospel, and do not declare the whole counsel of God. The result of unbelief and sin in others will fall on us if we do not warn them.

O sirs, if we are unfaithful, God will deal with us at the day of judgment, as He will deal with the wicked; this is an awful outlook for us. May we never dare to tone down the more severe parts of the story, and flatter men in their sins; for if we do this, God will mete out to us a portion with the condemned! If we have sown pillows for their armholes and rocked their cradles by our smooth speech, their eternal ruin shall lie at our door. How shall we bear it when God shall "do so to us, and more also," because we kept back His message from the sons of men who so much needed it?[7]

Moses didn't have the knowledge we possess. He didn't have the indwelling dynamic of the Holy Spirit as we do. He didn't yet have the Ten Commandments written by the finger of God or the revelation of Hell given to us by Jesus. Neither did he have the cross as evidence of God's great love. We have all these things, leaving us without excuse. If we offer excuses to Him, it's obvious that we haven't removed the shoes of our pride. We are more worried about ourselves and what people think of us than about those we are commanded to love.

CHAPTER *Five*

MOSES GOES
TO EGYPT

I n Luke 8:8, Jesus said something that was a little strange.
And He was impassioned as He said it:

> When He had said these things He cried, "He who has
> ears to hear, let him hear!"

He "cried" because what He had just said was of great
importance. His Parable of the Sower tells us that when the
gospel is preached, it results in genuine conversions and in
false conversions. Understanding this truth gives light to all
the parables that Jesus gave (see Mark 4:13). But the saying,
"He who has ears to hear, let him hear!" also holds depth of
meaning. It can be interpreted that the criteria for hearing
what Jesus taught is a level playing field for all of humanity.
All you need is to have ears, and everyone has ears. Even the
deaf have ears. They can "hear" what Jesus said, if they have a
mind to understand. The words can also mean that those
who hear Him should have a humble and teachable heart. A
listening ear, not just a mere physical ear. There were times
when He said things that not everyone was able to hear. This
was the case with celibacy. When it came to the subject of
divorce, Jesus went way back to Genesis:

The Pharisees also came to Him, testing Him, and saying to Him, "Is it lawful for a man to divorce his wife for just any reason?"

And He answered and said to them, "Have you not read that He who made them at the beginning 'made them male and female,' and said, 'For this reason a man shall leave his father and mother and be joined to his wife, and the two shall become one flesh'? So then, they are no longer two but one flesh. Therefore what God has joined together, let not man separate." (Matthew 19:3–6)

In doing so, Jesus drove a nail into the coffin of Darwinian evolution. *At the beginning God made them male and female.* Adam and Eve were made man and woman. They were made in the image of God, and therefore didn't have primates as an ancestor. Anyone who professes to be a Christian cannot embrace evolution and have faith in Jesus at the same time.

ANYONE WHO PROFESSES TO BE A CHRISTIAN CANNOT EMBRACE EVOLUTION AND HAVE FAITH IN JESUS AT THE SAME TIME.

The Pharisees then pointed to Moses to try to justify easy divorce:

They said to Him, "Why then did Moses command to give a certificate of divorce, and to put her away?"

He said to them, "Moses, because of the hardness of your hearts, permitted you to divorce your wives, but from the beginning it was not so. And I say to you, whoever divorces his wife, except for sexual immorality, and marries another, commits adultery; and whoever marries her who is divorced commits adultery."

His disciples said to Him, "If such is the case of the man with his wife, it is better not to marry." (Matthew 19:7–10)

Here is an important lesson from Scripture. Skeptics often point to incidents in the Bible and wrongly conclude that what they read is God's perfect will. For example, Lot once offered his daughters to a pack of ravenous homosexuals (see Genesis 19:1–11). That was his insane idea, not God's. Japheth offered his daughter as a sacrifice (see Judges 11:30–39). That was a crazy thing to do. Likewise, Moses allowing divorce was not the divine will. But God *permitted* it to be done. He permitted Lot to offer his daughters. He permitted Japheth to make his vow, and he permitted Moses to allow divorce because of the hardness of human hearts. As commentator David Guzik wrote, "It was as if Jesus said this: 'Here is the ideal; and here is the allowance of God when human sinfulness and hardness of heart has made the ideal unobtainable.'"[8]

Then Jesus qualified what He has just said:

"All cannot accept this saying, but only those to whom it has been given: For there are eunuchs who were born thus from their mother's womb, and there are eunuchs who were made eunuchs by men, and there are eunuchs who have made themselves eunuchs for the kingdom of heaven's sake. He who is able to accept it, let him accept it." (Matthew 19:11,12)

In other words, "He who has ears to hear, let him hear." When we open up the Law, our prayer is that sinners would have ears to hear the gospel. That's why, after presenting the gospel, I almost always ask, "Does what I have said make sense?" If it doesn't, I go through the Law again and speak of the fearfulness of falling into the hands of the living God. I want to take sinners by the shirt collar and pull their face close to mine and say, "*This is your precious life we are talking about! There is nothing more serious than being damned. Listen to me!*" But I can't do that because it would offend them. All I can do is to plead with God to open their ears to the truth of the gospel, and present it faithfully.

Charles Spurgeon said,

> There are many, who have ears, who do not hear to any real purpose. There is the physical act of hearing, but they do not hear in the heart and the mind. It is a very different thing to have an impression on the drum of the ear and to have an impression on the tablet of the heart.

FROM THE MOUNTAIN TO THE VALLEY

After his life-changing encounter with his Creator at the burning bush, Moses came down from his mountaintop experience to life as he knew it on earth. He'd been commissioned to take to his brethren the good news of freedom from bondage. Plus he had God's assurance that He would go with him, that his people would believe that I AM had sent him, and that Pharaoh would let the Hebrews go. It was simply a matter of speaking to the Pharaoh, and all would be well.

> So Moses went and returned to Jethro his father-in-law, and said to him, "Please let me go and return to my brethren who are in Egypt, and see whether they are still alive." And Jethro said to Moses, "Go in peace." (Exodus 4:18)

God even assured Moses that the danger he had fled from so many years earlier was gone:

Now the LORD said to Moses in Midian, "Go, return to Egypt; for all the men who sought your life are dead." Then Moses took his wife and his sons and set them on a donkey, and he returned to the land of Egypt. And Moses took the rod of God in his hand. (Exodus 4:19,20)

Moses had the rod of God in his hand, had received a divine reminder to use the rod to "do all those wonders," and on top of that he got an encouraging prophetic utterance:

And the LORD said to Moses, "When you go back to Egypt, see that you do all those wonders before Pharaoh which I have put in your hand. But I will harden his heart, so that he will not let the people go. Then you shall say to Pharaoh, 'Thus says the LORD: "Israel is My son, My firstborn. So I say to you, let My son go that he may serve Me. But if you refuse to let him go, indeed I will kill your son, your firstborn." ' " (Exodus 4:21–23)

God spoke to Aaron and told him to go to Moses. His brother then filled him in on what had happened. They gathered all the elders of the children of Israel, Aaron spoke all the words that the LORD had spoken to Moses, and then he did signs in the sight of the people. We are told:

So the people believed; and when they heard that the LORD had visited the children of Israel and that He had looked on their affliction, then they bowed their heads and worshiped. (Exodus 4:31)

The fear that Moses wouldn't be believed was completely unfounded. This was going to be a piece of cake.

Afterward Moses and Aaron went in and told Pharaoh, "Thus says the LORD God of Israel: 'Let My people go, that they may hold a feast to Me in the wilderness.'"

And Pharaoh said, "Who is the LORD, that I should obey His voice to let Israel go? I do not know the LORD, nor will I let Israel go." So they said, "The God of the Hebrews has met with us. Please, let us go three days' journey into the desert and sacrifice to the LORD our God, lest He fall upon us with pestilence or with the sword." (Exodus 5:1–3)

It was happening just as God said it would: Pharaoh was hardening his sinful heart. The same sun that hardens clay also melts butter. But then something unforetold happened. It was a curveball.

Then the king of Egypt said to them, "Moses and Aaron, why do you take the people from their work? Get back to your labor." And Pharaoh said, "Look, the people of the land are many now, and you make them rest from their labor!"

So the same day Pharaoh commanded the taskmasters of the people and their officers, saying, "You shall no longer give the people straw to make brick as before. Let them go and gather straw for themselves. And you shall lay on them the quota of bricks which they made before. You shall not reduce it. For they are idle; therefore they cry out, saying, 'Let us go and sacrifice to our God.' Let more work be laid on the men, that they may labor in it, and let them not regard false words." (Exodus 5:4–9)

After pleading with the Pharaoh and getting nowhere, the officers of the children of Israel said to Moses and Aaron:

"Let the LORD look on you and judge, because you have made us abhorrent in the sight of Pharaoh and in the sight of his servants, to put a sword in their hand to kill us." (vv. 20,21)

As far as the elders of Israel were concerned, all this happened because of Moses and Aaron. They stirred up the demons in Pharaoh, and now their people were suffering because those two opened their big mouths. Things were worse because of these contentious do-gooders. Years later Solomon wrote,

The beginning of strife is like releasing water; therefore stop contention before a quarrel starts. (Proverbs 17:14)

Now there was a flood of even more suffering for the children of Israel. A disgruntled Moses returned to the Lord and said,

"LORD, why have You brought trouble on this people? Why is it You have sent me? For since I came to Pharaoh to speak in Your name, he has done evil to this people; neither have You delivered Your people at all." (Exodus 5:22,23)

It all seemed so simple. Now it was a mess.

ME AND MY BIG MOUTH

Perhaps you have swallowed your fears and stepped out in faith—trusting the Lord by being obedient to the Great Commission. Maybe you shared the gospel with a coworker and nothing happened. Or worse, he complained to the management and now your job is on the line. You told your wife and she wondered why you had to go and open your mouth. You have kids to feed. You should have thought this through before you did this. Or perhaps you took courage and shared the gospel with your dear mother. She listened and seemed quite congenial, but you heard from your brother afterward that she was very upset about what you said. She now believes you think she's an evil person. This upset your churchgoing brother, and he told your other siblings. One of them informed you that your mom is definitely a good person. Your atheist sister burst into tears on the phone, asking what sort of evil person you are to think that your mother should go to Hell. Now you feel like you are the black sheep of your family. The very ones you wanted to reach have pushed you out of reach. You are wondering where God was in all this, and if you should have kept your mouth closed.

All this isn't supposed to be what happens when you're obedient. Or is it? Perhaps this is normal when God is at work. He wasn't caught by surprise when Pharaoh turned nasty.

Think of what happened with Stephen. God opened an amazing door for him to share the gospel with the Jewish leaders:

> Then the high priest said, "Are these things so?" And he [Stephen] said, "Brethren and fathers, listen: The God of glory appeared to our father Abraham when he was in Mesopotamia, before he dwelt in Haran, and said to him, 'Get out of your country and from your relatives, and come to a land that I will show you.'" (Acts 7:1–3)

And away went faithful Stephen, preaching an amazing message of God's grace in sending Jesus to die for a sinful world. But instead of being pricked to the heart, they were cut to the heart and murdered him:

> Then they cried out with a loud voice, stopped their ears, and ran at him with one accord; and they cast him out of the city and stoned him. (Acts 7:57,58)

That devastated the church. That wasn't supposed to happen. Then things got even worse:

> Now Saul was consenting to his death. At that time a great persecution arose against the church which was at Jerusalem; and they were all scattered throughout the regions of Judea and Samaria, except the apostles. And devout men carried Stephen to his burial, and made great lamentation over him. As for Saul, he made havoc of the church, entering every house, and dragging off men and women, committing them to prison. (Acts 8:1–3)

Where was God in all this terrible chaos? He said that He would always be with them. The answer was that He was working behind the scenes, as He did with Moses.

Or think of Paul and Silas. They had gone into all the world as they were commanded to. They were faithfully preaching the gospel when a demon-possessed woman took a liking to them. She started following them and yelling out that people should listen to them. Paul finally had had enough and cast out the demon:

> And they brought them to the magistrates, and said, "These men, being Jews, exceedingly trouble our city; and they teach customs which are not lawful for us, being Romans, to receive or observe." Then the multitude rose up together against them; and the magistrates tore off their clothes and commanded them to be beaten with rods. And when they had laid many stripes on them, they threw them into prison, commanding the jailer to keep them securely. Having received such a charge, he put them into the inner prison and fastened their feet in the stocks. (Acts 16:20–24)

Paul and Silas were beaten and then tossed into a cold prison. Where was God in all this chaos? It made no sense. Again, He was working behind the scenes, as He did with Stephen, and as He did with Moses.

Then of course there was the horror of the cross. We glory in it because we see it from this side, but could you imagine being one of the disciples during the dark hours surrounding the crucifixion? They were still in an unregenerate state—not like those of us who have been born again, whose understanding has been enlightened. Jesus called two of them fools and slow of heart to believe the Scriptures (see Luke 24:25). They abandoned Jesus when He was arrested, no doubt thinking this wasn't the way things should be going.

NOT THE SMALLEST SEED IS LOST IF GOD SEES FIT TO CAUSE IT TO GROW. HE GIVES THE INCREASE.

But God was with Jesus. Nothing was going haywire. It was all going according to the divine plan, even though nothing was making sense to the disciples. He was working behind the scenes, as He did with Paul and Silas, as He did with Stephen, and as He did with Moses.

And He's working behind the scenes with you, no matter how dark and chaotic things may seem with those to whom you faithfully give the gospel. Not the smallest seed is lost if God sees fit to cause it to grow. He gives the increase. This is why Scripture reminds us to "be steadfast, immovable, always abounding in the work of the Lord, knowing that your labor is not in vain in the Lord" (1 Corinthians 15:58).

In one sense it's understandable that Moses said, "LORD, why have You brought trouble on this people? Why is it You have sent me?" (Exodus 5:22). He didn't have the comfort of the Scriptures. He didn't have the knowledge that we have, that no matter how dark the day, the sun of God's faithfulness still shines. He didn't have Hebrews 11 as we have, giving us a list of faithful heroes who trusted God in times of trouble because they, like Moses, saw Him who is invisible (see Hebrews 11:27).

DEAL WITH THIS

When Moses complained to the LORD that things were not going as planned, God said, "Now you shall see what I will do to Pharaoh. For with a strong hand he will let them go, and with a strong hand he will drive them out of his land" (Exodus 6:1).

Moses had stepped out in faith, trusting God's promises, and "faith is the substance of things hoped for, the evidence of things not seen" (Hebrews 11:1). He trusted without seeing. But now he had God's word that he would see. Now he would witness I AM manifesting His great power. Look at the surety of this promise:

> And God spoke to Moses and said to him: "I am the LORD. I appeared to Abraham, to Isaac, and to Jacob, as God Almighty, but by My name LORD I was not known to them. I have also established My covenant with them, to give them the land of Canaan, the land of their pilgrimage, in which they were strangers. And I have also heard the groaning of the children of Israel whom the Egyptians keep in bondage, and I have remembered My covenant. Therefore say to the children of Israel: 'I am the LORD; I will bring you out from under the burdens of the Egyptians, I will rescue you from their bondage, and I will redeem you with an outstretched

81

arm and with great judgments. I will take you as My people, and I will be your God. Then you shall know that I am the LORD your God who brings you out from under the burdens of the Egyptians. And I will bring you into the land which I swore to give to Abraham, Isaac, and Jacob; and I will give it to you as a heritage: I am the LORD.'" (Exodus 6:2–8)

The great I AM reminds Moses:

- Who He is
- What He has done with Moses' forefathers
- Of the immutable covenant He made with them
- That He has heard the groaning of the children of Israel and remembered His covenant

Then He said to tell them:

"I will bring you out...I will rescue you...I will redeem you...I will take you as My people...I will be your God...I will bring you into the land...I will give it to you as a heritage."

Seven times God said, "I will." *This was going to happen.*

So Moses spoke thus to the children of Israel; but they did not heed Moses, because of anguish of spirit and cruel bondage. (Exodus 6:9)

Moses gave the seven assurances that God would rescue them, but they didn't believe that He would keep His word. So God spoke to Moses and said, "Go in, tell Pharaoh king of Egypt to let the children of Israel go out of his land" (v. 11). Then Moses said, "The children of Israel have not heeded me. How then shall Pharaoh heed me, for I am of uncircumcised lips?" (v. 12). But look at this:

> Then Moses and Aaron did so; just as the LORD commanded them, so they did. (Exodus 7:6)

And there is our great lesson: "For whatever things were written before were written for our learning, that we through the patience and comfort of the Scriptures might have hope" (Romans 15:4). Do you identify with the fear to which Moses continually clung? I do. I have mounted a soapbox thousands of times to preach to the unsaved. I have witnessed one-to-one countless times for over forty-five years, yet I am as insecure as Moses. And I'm not getting better as I get older. Fear plagues me. And so I take comfort in his weakness and in his pleading with God to bypass him as a spokesman. I take comfort that I am normal when fear makes me tremble.

But at the same time I see that in his weakness Moses still obeyed. And that is the essence of love. It overcomes the tormenting fear. It makes weakness its strength. Fear makes me pray. It makes me trust God, because I can't do this task by myself. Moses loved his people and he loved His Creator. In his weakness he trusted God, and that made him strong:

> By faith Moses, when he was born, was hidden three months by his parents, because they saw he was a beautiful child; and they were not afraid of the king's command.

By faith Moses, when he became of age, refused to be called the son of Pharaoh's daughter, choosing rather to suffer affliction with the people of God than to enjoy the passing pleasures of sin, esteeming the reproach of Christ greater riches than the treasures in Egypt; for he looked to the reward.

By faith he forsook Egypt, not fearing the wrath of the king; for he endured as seeing Him who is invisible. By faith he kept the Passover and the sprinkling of blood, lest he who destroyed the firstborn should touch them.

By faith they passed through the Red Sea as by dry land, whereas the Egyptians, attempting to do so, were drowned. (Hebrews 11:23–29)

Take, as another example, rugby legend Israel Folau. He was Australian rugby's greatest player, and he was unashamed of his faith in Jesus. One day in April 2019 someone on social media asked him what would happen to homosexuals on Judgment Day. Israel answered with Scripture, by listing those who would not enter Heaven.

CNN reported:

Australian rugby union star Israel Folau has been sacked after he posted an anti-gay statement on social media.

A devout Christian who has made 73 international appearances for the Wallabies, Folau was found guilty of a code of conduct breach last week, following a homophobic social media post, which listed "drunks, homosexuals, adulterers, liars, fornicators, thieves, atheists and idolaters," reading underneath, "Hell awaits you."

The controversial Instagram post in April has not been deleted.[9]

The hateful and intolerant liberal media of course went crazy, calling him hateful and intolerant. But at the same time, they kept quoting the list, along with other Bible verses, as well as stating that Folau had said that everyone on the list needed to repent and trust Jesus. Suddenly, multitudes of godless people began conversations about who will and who won't enter Heaven. God wonderfully used this chaotic situation to bring the gospel to the ungodly.

Therefore, never let fear stop you from trusting God. You will never know what would have been if you let it paralyze you.

CHAPTER Six

THROW IT DOWN

M oses and Aaron now find themselves on the front line of battle. God had prepared them for this by saying, "When Pharaoh speaks to you, saying, 'Show a miracle for yourselves,' then you shall say to Aaron, 'Take your rod and cast it before Pharaoh, and let it become a serpent'" (Exodus 7:8,9). Once again, things don't go as planned. I'm sure they didn't expect Egypt's magicians to do what they did:

> So Moses and Aaron went in to Pharaoh, and they did so, just as the LORD commanded. And Aaron cast down his rod before Pharaoh and before his servants, and it became a serpent.
>
> But Pharaoh also called the wise men and the sorcerers; so the magicians of Egypt, they also did in like manner with their enchantments. For every man threw down his rod, and they became serpents. But Aaron's rod swallowed up their rods. (Exodus 7:9–12)

No matter what argument the world throws at your feet, the rod of God's Law will swallow it whole. Never forget this miraculous weapon God has placed into your hands. It is "mighty in God for pulling down strongholds" (2 Corinthians 10:4). When a disbelieving world casts down accusations about God being tyrannical, or questions about suffering, hypocrisy, or evolution, or claims that there's no evidence for God, answer their questions briefly if you can, then swing to the conscience with the Law. Do what Jesus did.

When certain people came to Him with questions about suffering and evil, He said, "Do you suppose that these Galileans were worse sinners than all other Galileans, because they suffered such things? I tell you, no; but unless you repent you will all likewise perish" (Luke 13:2,3). Suddenly sinners' concerns about God's dealings with others were turned back to their own sin that would take them to Hell, unless they repented. The Law was given to stop every mouth. It swallows up sinner's excuses and leaves them guilty before God (see Romans 3:19,20).

Here is the full quote from Charles Spurgeon that so impacted me back in 1982. Watch him plague the sinner with the Law:

> But more, there is war between you and God's Law. The Ten Commandments are against you . . . The First one comes forward and says, "Let him be cursed, for he denies me. He has another god besides me; his god is his belly, he yields homage to his lust." All the Ten Commandments, like ten great pieces of cannon, are pointed at you today, for you have broken all God's statutes, and lived in the daily neglect of all His commands. Soul! You will find it a hard thing to go to war with the Law. When the Law came in peace, Sinai was altogether on a smoke, and even Moses said, "I do exceedingly fear and quake." What will you do when the Law comes in terror, when the trumpet of the archangel shall tear you from your grave, when the eyes of God shall burn their way

into your guilty soul, when the great books shall be opened, and all your sin and shame shall be published? Can you stand against an angry law in that day?[10]

Spurgeon eloquently put into words the breathtakingly fearful experience of falling into the hands of the living God. We may long to be able to reason with sinners with such persuasion, but we can take consolation; though the Prince of Preachers was blessed with an eloquent tongue, we needn't long for that gift. Moses didn't have it. Neither did Paul use his brilliance. Remember, he said that his speech and preaching "were not with persuasive words of human wisdom, but in demonstration of the Spirit and of power" (1 Corinthians 2:4). Again, don't fall into the trap of pleading inadequacy. We are able to speak boldly because the power of our persuasion is in the gospel and in the fact that I AM is with us.

GOD KEPT HIS WORD

Moses was made "as God to Pharaoh" (Exodus 7:1). He spoke and plagues fell on Egypt.

Let me again allow Spurgeon to help us here. Listen to him make sense of Pharaoh and these plagues:

PHARAOH is the type and image of proud men. God permitted him to be left to the natural hardness of his heart, and he stood up against Jehovah in a very remarkable way. Those who are students of the ancient history of Egypt, those especially who have seen the remains of the colossal statues of the kings, and those tremendous pyramids which probably were the places of their sepulture, will know that man worship was carried on to the very highest degree in connection with the ancient kingdom of Egypt.

Our modern civilization has deprived kings of much of the dignity which once hedged them round. We have grown wonderfully familiar with our fellow men in the very highest places of the earth, but in those old monarchies, when the king was absolute and supreme, when his wish, even though he was little better than a maniac —was the law that governed the people—when not a dog dared move his tongue against the despot, then kings seemed to be like little gods, and they lorded it over their subjects with a vengeance! No doubt they grew intoxicated with the fumes of the incense which their subjects willingly offered to them, and so came to think themselves almost, if not quite, divine—and assumed the position and honors of God, Himself.

It is not so very amazing, therefore, that Pharaoh should have thought that, in the God of the Hebrews, he had merely met with just another one of the same stamp as himself, against whom he could carry on war, and whom he might even subdue. He said within himself, "Who are these Hebrews? Their fathers were a company of shepherds who came and settled in Egypt! And as for these people, they are my slaves! I have built cities with their unpaid labor, and I mean to hold them in captivity. They talk about their God, their 'Jehovah.' Who is Jehovah that I should obey His voice? Let it be a battle of Pharaoh against Jehovah, and let it be fought out to the bitter end! I will show these people that I care not for them, or their prophets, or their God."[11]

With the thought that Pharaoh represents the pride of man, we can see how the ten plagues represent the Ten Commandments, plaguing proud sinners and bringing them to their sinful knees.

Moses had been given a glimpse of the future, and because he knew what was coming, he warned Pharaoh of the terrible consequences of hardening his heart against the Lord.

We are ambassadors for Christ and have been given a glimpse of the fearful future. God Himself speaks through us when we preach His gospel:

> Now all things are of God, who has reconciled us to Himself through Jesus Christ, and has given us the ministry of reconciliation, that is, that God was in Christ reconciling the world to Himself, not imputing their trespasses to them, and has committed to us the word of reconciliation.
>
> Now then, we are ambassadors for Christ, as though God were pleading through us: we implore you on Christ's behalf, be reconciled to God. (2 Corinthians 5:18–20)

We warn every man because we want to present every man perfect in Christ Jesus (Colossians 1:28). But they won't come to the cross when there's pride in their heart, and neither will they come while they cling to their beloved sins. It is the plague of the Law that persuades them that if they want to live, they must obey the gospel by repenting and trusting in the blood of the Lamb.

God then spoke to Moses about what to do to be saved from death:

> "And they shall take some of the blood and put it on the two doorposts and on the lintel of the houses where they eat it . . .
>
> "For I will pass through the land of Egypt on that night, and will strike all the firstborn in the land of Egypt, both man and beast; and against all the gods of

Egypt I will execute judgment: I am the LORD. Now the blood shall be a sign for you on the houses where you are. And when I see the blood, I will pass over you; and the plague shall not be on you to destroy you when I strike the land of Egypt." (Exodus 12:7,12,13)

Moses took that sobering message, called for all the elders of Israel, and said to them:

"Pick out and take lambs for yourselves according to your families, and kill the Passover lamb. And you shall take a bunch of hyssop, dip it in the blood that is in the basin, and strike the lintel and the two doorposts with the blood that is in the basin. And none of you shall go out of the door of his house until morning. For the LORD will pass through to strike the Egyptians; and when He sees the blood on the lintel and on the two doorposts, the LORD will pass over the door and not allow the destroyer to come into your houses to strike you." (Exodus 12:21–23)

And so death brought the final and most terrifying plague to Egypt. Nine loving and patient warnings didn't humble nor persuade Pharaoh. It took a deathblow to do that. The death of his beloved firstborn broke his stubborn pride.

Oh, how stubborn this world is. Plague after plague falls upon them in this life. Each suffering is a sober and loving warning, soaked in the patience of God as He holds back His wrath, that He means what He says about sin. It is *deadly* serious. Life, with all its suffering, should humble the unsaved, but more often than not it doesn't. They need to be plagued by the Law so that it kills their beloved firstborn. Whatever inordinate love they cling to must die. Whatever they put before their love for God must be put to death before they can be saved. Some refuse, cling to their idol, and walk away sorrowful, as did the rich young ruler:

> Now as He was going out on the road, one came running, knelt before Him, and asked Him, "Good Teacher, what shall I do that I may inherit eternal life?"
>
> So Jesus said to him, "Why do you call Me good? No one is good but One, that is, God. You know the commandments: 'Do not commit adultery,' 'Do not murder,' 'Do not steal,' 'Do not bear false witness,' 'Do not defraud,' 'Honor your father and your mother.'"
>
> And he answered and said to Him, "Teacher, all these things I have kept from my youth."
>
> Then Jesus, looking at him, loved him, and said to him, "One thing you lack: Go your way, sell whatever you have and give to the poor, and you will have treasure in heaven; and come, take up the cross, and follow Me."
>
> But he was sad at this word, and went away sorrowful, for he had great possessions. (Mark 10:17–22)

It was the Law that showed the man his sin. He had another god before His Creator. He loved his money, and you cannot serve God and money (Matthew 6:24). His firstborn love had to die before he could come to the cross. And the miracle is that those who forsake their first love find a passionate love for God when they are born again.

I think of the grip that surfing had on me the day before I came to the cross. The night I was saved, I let it go, and the next morning I didn't even want to go surfing. Inordinate love had gone. That astounded me. I was no longer a slave to my desires. I could take it or leave it because I was free to do so. It was a relief, because the pleasure it gave me was bound in the admiration of men. I wanted to win contests so that I would be well-known. I wanted the praise of men, but salvation caused me to want only the praise of God ... and I found His smile in Christ. I tremble to think what futility I would have chased over the last forty years if I hadn't put surfing on the altar. I would have wasted thousands of hours floating on water. Instead, I have served God and have the satisfaction that I haven't wasted my years. Do the same. Play your sport, go to your gym, travel the world, chase your dreams, but let all these things be secondary to living to reach the lost for the glory of God. That's what it means to number your days and apply your heart to wisdom (Psalm 90:12).

THE RED SEA

The Law plagues sinners and drives them to the edge of the Red Sea—to a place of helpless hopelessness. It leaves them with nowhere to go but to God. It puts them between the rock of a chasing taskmaster and a hard place of no escape. When all hope seems to be gone, Moses points his finger to a living hope. He says, "Stand still and see the salvation of God!"

The Law, in its unrelenting wrath, in its terrible condemnation, suddenly becomes a guiding teacher. The light from its lightning reveals the cross. The thunder of its wrath awakens us to grace. God in His great love and mercy gave the Law as a tutor to bring us to Christ:

> But before faith came, we were kept under guard by the law, kept for the faith which would afterward be revealed. Therefore the law was our tutor to bring us to Christ, that we might be justified by faith. But after faith has come, we are no longer under a tutor. (Galatians 3:23–25)

It is when we stand still in helpless humility that the wind of mercy blows. Mercy opens the way of escape from what seemed to be certain death:

And can it be that I should gain
An interest in the Savior's blood?
Died He for me, who caused His pain?
For me, who Him to death pursued?[12]

How could it be that brilliant light appeared in my gross darkness! Oh, happy day, when Jesus washed my sins away. Thanks be to God for the unwarranted, unexpected, and unspeakable gift of eternal life. The enemy was overcome by the Captain of our Salvation. The grave lost its deadly sting and death lost its victory! Jesus destroyed death at the cross. We can now walk through the valley of the shadow of death and fear no evil.

GOD IN HIS GREAT LOVE AND MERCY GAVE THE LAW AS A TUTOR TO BRING US TO CHRIST.

Without Jesus we are without hope of escaping Hell. "How shall we escape if we neglect so great a salvation?" (Hebrews 2:3). And the world will neglect the gospel, as long as their love for sin is more prevalent than their awareness of danger. Crows will peck at a carcass until the last second as a truck approaches, and sinners who think they can escape damnation will peck at sin until the truck strikes them.

But the Law reaches its long arm down into their heart and reveals that God requires truth in the inward parts. When lust, hatred, covetousness, lying, stealing, ingratitude, and blasphemy beckon the vehicle of eternal justice, they suddenly see the wisdom of fleeing from the rotting carcass of sin.

MORE IMPORTANT THAN HAPPINESS

In our unregenerate state, sin deceives us into thinking that it is the oxygen by which we live. The devil whispers that a life without lust would be a life without pleasure. To give up sin is to let go of the last semblance of happiness in this miserable world. And so it is easier to get a tender T-bone from the jaws of a hungry dog than for a sin-loving sinner to let go of his sins.

How then do we use the Law to get the dog to drop the bone? In the following real-life witnessing encounter, transcribed from our YouTube channel, I approached Kilany as he sat on a park bench.

Ray: Is there anything more important than happiness?

Kilany: Not really, no. I mean, loving your family, friends, and everyone else.

R: Have you ever heard of the word "righteousness"?

K: Yes.

R: Do you know what it means? It's a biblical word, usually not one we use in everyday talk, but it's used a lot in Scripture. Do you know what it means?

K: Not exactly.

R: It means "that which is right." Do you think that is more important than happiness?

K: No.

R: Let's say that rape makes a man happy or robbing a bank makes him happy.

K: No, no, no!

R: So righteousness is more important than happiness, and it's a word that our lives depend on actually. Did you realize that your whole life depends on the word righteousness?

K: No.

R: While this life depends on oxygen, the oxygen of eternity is righteousness. That's what the Bible says: "Riches do not profit in the day of wrath, but righteousness delivers from death." Do you know what that verse means?

K: No.

R: I'll explain it to you in a roundabout way. Do you think you are a good person?

K: Yes.

R: I'm going to show you that you need righteousness, okay? More than you need oxygen that you breathe. How many lies have you told in your life?

K: Man, you don't even know. Sometimes you don't even know what you are doing, so I would have to lie.

R: Have you ever stolen something?

K: Have I ever stolen something? Stolen a quarter from my brother.

R: You know, when people repeat the question it means they are backing up and thinking of a way out. Have you ever stolen something? Other than a quarter from your brother? If you take a dollar out of my wallet it's as much theft as if you take $100 out of my wallet. Have you ever used God's name in vain?

K: No.

R: "OMG"?

K: Oh. Well, you know, it happens. I go [blasphemy].

R: Jesus said that if you look at a woman and lust after her, you have committed adultery with her in your heart. Have you looked at a woman with lust?

K: It has happened before.

R: So, Kilany, I am not judging you, but you just told me you are a lying, thieving, blasphemous adulterer at heart. And you've got to face God on Judgment Day. If He judges you by the Ten Commandments (we've looked at four), are you going be innocent or guilty?

K: I'd be guilty.

R: Heaven or Hell?

K: That's His choice.

R: He says that all liars will have their part in the lake of fire. No thief, no blasphemer, no adulterer will inherit the Kingdom of God. Have you had sex outside of marriage?

K: Yes.

R: That's fornication. The Bible says no fornicators will inherit the Kingdom of God. How can you be made right with God? Where can you get righteousness from?

K: Church. Not only church, but living through God every day. Following what He tells you to do. Looking at His signs, listening—read the Bible regularly... just living through God and following His rules.

R: You said everything except the right answer. The right answer is that God provided a Savior, Jesus of Nazareth —a perfect sinless Man who suffered and died on a cross to take the punishment for the sin of the world. You probably know that, but you may not know this aspect. You and I broke God's Law—the moral Law, the Ten Commandments—and Jesus came and paid the fine in full. If you are in court and someone pays the fine, the judge can let you go. It can be legal and merciful at the same time. He can say, "This man is guilty, but someone has paid his fine; he is out of here." God can extend mercy toward you and satisfy justice because your fine was paid by Jesus on the cross.

The Bible says that God "made Him who knew no sin to be sin for us, that we might become the righteousness of God in Him." So God can make you righteous by His grace, by His mercy. Remember, "Riches do not profit in the day of wrath, but *righteousness* delivers from death." So you need a right standing with God. You need to be justified and made right with God, and the only way you can do that is by trusting in Him who suffered on the cross for the sins of the world and rose from the dead on the third day. So what do you have to do to get right with God? Do you know the way of salvation?

K: No, not really.

R: The Bible says that God commands all men everywhere to repent. And the Scripture says, if you put your faith in Jesus, God will remit your sins; He will forgive you, justify you, and make you righteous. In the same way that, if you put your faith in a parachute when you are going to jump 10,000 feet, that parachute will save your life, so the

Bible says to "put on the Lord Jesus Christ," to repent and trust in Him. Say, "God, I've been like Adam, hiding from you, like a criminal from the police. I've loved the darkness, I've hated the light, but I come out to the light today." Say, "God, please change my heart. I need to be born again. I need my sins forgiven, I need the righteousness of Christ." The Bible says that He is faithful and He promised He will forgive your sins in an instant if you repent and trust in Christ. So when are you going to do that—get right with God?

K: I've been trying to get right with God.

R: Today, if you hear His voice, don't harden your heart. Does that make sense?

K: Yes.

R: So are you willing to give up your sinful ways—the love of pornography, fornication, and all those things—and say, "God, change me"?

K: Everyday life. You know, sometimes you go through things and it's like, you try so hard to get on track and stay on an unsinful life but, you know. The way life is...

R: It's not going to happen without the help of God. So that's what happens when you are born again—you receive the Holy Spirit. You are surrounded by temptations that other generations didn't have. You can have instant pornography in seconds that will mess up your mind and bring God's anger upon yourself, because you are violating His Law through lust. These temptations are all around us, and when you become a Christian you've got to grab that Bible verse that says, "No temptation has

100

overtaken you except such as is common to man." Everyone gets temptations. But God is faithful, and will provide the way of escape, that you may be able to bear it. So, get right with God, trust in Jesus, read your Bible daily, obey what you read, and He will never let you down. Does that make sense?

K: Yes.

R: Can I pray with you?

K: All right.

THE LAW AND THE CHRISTIAN

We have looked at the power of the Law of Moses to act as a tutor to bring us to Christ. But its amazing work doesn't stop there. It not only brings us to the cross, it keeps us there. Listen to Spurgeon wonderfully address this point:

> Again, the Law is written in the heart *by repentance working hatred of sin*. Burnt children, you know, are afraid of the fire. Oh, what a horror I have had of sin ever since the day when I felt its power over my soul! It was enough to drive me mad when I felt the guilt of sin; it would have done so, I sometimes think, if I had continued much longer in that terrible condition. O sin, *sin*, I have had enough of you! You never brought me more than a moment's seeming joy, and with it there came a deep and awful bitterness which burns within me to this day! And now, being set free from sin, can I go back to it? Some of you, my brethren and sisters, came to Christ with such difficulty that you were saved, as it were, by the skin of your teeth. You were like Jonah, you had to come up from the bottom of the mountains, and out of the very belly of hell you cried unto God.

Well, that experience has made sin so bitter to you that you will not go back to it. The Law has been written in your heart with the steel pen of repentance, and God has made sin to be a horrible evil to you.[13]

Moses did us a great service by bearing the great tablets of the Law, written by the finger of God. He opened our eyes to what Paul described as the exceeding sinfulness of sin:

> For sin, seizing its opportunity through the commandment, beguiled and completely deceived me, and using it as a weapon killed me [separating me from God]. So then, the Law is holy, and the commandment is holy and righteous and good.
>
> Did that which is good [the Law], then become death to me? Certainly not! But sin, in order that it might be revealed as sin, was producing death in me by [using] this good thing [as a weapon], so that through the commandment sin would become exceedingly sinful. (Romans 7:11–13, AMP)

When the callous rich man found himself tormented in Hell, he asked for Abraham to send someone to warn his brothers. But Abraham pointed to Moses:

> Abraham said to him, 'They have Moses and the prophets; let them hear them.' And he said, 'No, father Abraham; but if one goes to them from the dead, they will repent.' But he said to him, '*If they do not hear Moses* and the prophets, neither will they be persuaded though one rise from the dead.'" (Luke 16:30,31)

Do the same. It is such an important truth—that sinners need to hear Moses or they won't be persuaded though one rise from the dead. Millions may believe that Jesus conquered death through the cross and rose again, but they're still unsaved if they've never repented of their sin and trusted in Jesus alone for their eternal salvation. Moses shows them that they are sinners. Without the Law of Moses, Paul said that he didn't even know what sin was: "I would not have known sin except through the law" (Romans 7:7).

PILLAR OF FIRE

And the Angel of God, who went before the camp of Israel, moved and went behind them; and the pillar of cloud went from before them and stood behind them. So it came between the camp of the Egyptians and the camp of Israel. Thus it was a cloud and darkness to the one, and it gave light by night to the other, so that the one did not come near the other all that night. (Exodus 14:19,20)

I rarely read of the pillar of fire without being taken back to my high school days. It was a secular school, but for some reason we sang Christian hymns in our morning assemblies, and one of these famous hymns mentioned that pillar. I was unsaved and didn't have a clue as to the beauty and truth of these words:

Guide me, O Thou great Jehovah,
Pilgrim through this barren land.
I am weak but Thou art mighty;
Hold me with Thy powerful hand.
Bread of Heaven,
Bread of Heaven,
Feed me till I want no more;
Feed me till I want no more.
Open now the crystal fountain

Whence the healing stream doth flow;
Let the fiery, cloudy pillar
Lead me all my journey through.[14]

I often quietly sing this hymn while looking for people to witness to. It's my prayer that God would guide me to those whose hearts He has prepared, something I often see happen.

The Christian lives in a supernatural realm of which unbelievers are unaware. We are guided through life by the fiery, cloudy pillar. To us, the Christian walk is like that fiery, cloudy pillar. It is "a cloud and darkness" to the unbelieving world, and at the same time it gives "light by night" to the believer. To the humble who trust in the Savior, the Scriptures are the very will and voice of God that give daily direction and moral guidance. They are filled with life lessons and exceedingly great and precious promises on which believers rest our faith, gain assurance of immortality, and conquer the fear of death. The Bible is a lamp to our feet and a light to our path.

But to the proud of heart, the Bible is nothing but a confusing cloud of darkness, and the glorious light of the gospel is nothing but darkened foolishness. All the great truths—of faith, of righteousness, of repentance, justification, forgiveness, etc.—are hidden from the proud.

Faith to the Christian is the means of exchange between him and his Creator. He joyfully believes every precious promise of God. To the unbeliever, faith is for weak and unthinking people who blindly believe despite evidence to the contrary.

"Righteousness" to the Christian is his hope for eternity. He knows that God loves righteousness and that without a right standing with Him, he will perish on the Day of Wrath.

But to the sinner, his own happiness trumps righteousness, and he lives his life accordingly with no fear of divine retribution. It is because of this willful blindness that he vainly seeks justification though self-righteousness and thinks that repentance is all that's needed to find peace with God...if there is some issue of wrongdoing. Everything to do with God is nebulous and cloudy. And tragedy of tragedies, the greatest news that any human being could ever hope to hear —that the gift of God is eternal life (Romans 6:23)—is not good news at all. It is discarded as irrelevant:

> But even if our gospel is veiled, it is veiled to those who are perishing, whose minds the god of this age has blinded, who do not believe, lest the light of the gospel of the glory of Christ, who is the image of God, should shine on them. (2 Corinthians 4:3,4)

THE CHRISTIAN LIVES IN A SUPERNATURAL REALM OF WHICH UNBELIEVERS ARE UNAWARE.

Once again, it is no mystery as to why the gospel is foolishness to a proud heart. The reason is that the good news of a fine being paid by another on my behalf is senseless *if I don't believe I have broken any law.* This is such an important point for those who want to reach the lost. Every demon in Hell will clamp his cold and bony fingers over your eyes and ears to stop you from seeing this truth.

Could you get excited if I told you that a fine had been paid for you when you believe that you have always been law-abiding? The thought is not only irrelevant, it's offensive. Mentioning a fine being paid on your behalf says that you have committed an unlawful act, when you think you haven't. This is why the moral Law must be applied to the conscience. The knowledge of sin will humble the proud heart, show the terrible danger, and cause sinners see the light of the glorious gospel of Jesus Christ.

> Then Moses stretched out his hand over the sea; and the LORD caused the sea to go back by a strong east wind all that night, and made the sea into dry land, and the waters were divided. So the children of Israel went into the midst of the sea on the dry ground, and the waters were a wall to them on their right hand and on their left. And the Egyptians pursued and went after them into the midst of the sea, all Pharaoh's horses, his chariots, and his horsemen. (Exodus 14:21–23)

Here is the climax of the promise of God to deliver His people. Moses had seen the miraculous plagues that God poured upon Pharaoh. Now I AM, the Creator of the universe, had miraculously opened up the Red Sea.

> Now it came to pass, in the morning watch, that the LORD looked down upon the army of the Egyptians through the pillar of fire and cloud, and He troubled the army of the Egyptians. And He took off their chariot wheels, so that they drove them with difficulty; and the Egyptians said, "Let us flee from the face of Israel, for the LORD fights for them against the Egyptians."
>
> Then the LORD said to Moses, "Stretch out your hand over the sea, that the waters may come back upon the Egyptians, on their chariots, and on their horsemen." And Moses stretched out his hand over the sea; and when the morning appeared, the sea returned to its full depth, while the Egyptians were fleeing into it. So

the LORD overthrew the Egyptians in the midst of the sea. Then the waters returned and covered the chariots, the horsemen, and all the army of Pharaoh that came into the sea after them. Not so much as one of them remained. But the children of Israel had walked on dry land in the midst of the sea, and the waters were a wall to them on their right hand and on their left. (Exodus 14:24–29)

The ungodly think that they will follow us into Heaven. After all, they are as good as, if not better than, any Christian. They believe in God; they have made mistakes, made wrong choices, maybe sinned a little here and there, but it's no big deal. Any lies have been little and any theft has been petty. Besides, that was in the past. God is merciful and kind; He's not this petty judge that Christians portray Him to be. Who are they to judge anyway? Doesn't the Bible say, "Judge not, that you be not judged" (Matthew 7:1)? They are hypocrites to point the finger.

One who is ignorant believes God will let him into Heaven, because he thinks he's a good person at heart. But the great weight of the Law is going to fall on him. No one is going to cross over who isn't trusting in the blood of the spotless Lamb. The Scriptures warn "there shall by no means enter it anything that defiles, or causes an abomination or a lie, but only those who are written in the Lamb's Book of Life" (Revelation 21:27). No one will pass through who is sexually immoral or embraces idolatry (see Revelation 22:15).

So the LORD saved Israel that day out of the hand of the Egyptians, and Israel saw the Egyptians dead on the seashore. Thus Israel saw the great work which the LORD had done in Egypt; so the people feared the LORD, and believed the LORD and His servant Moses. (Exodus 14:30,31)

I was on my bike waiting at the edge of a very busy road. It was a little frustrating because there was so many cars coming from the left and from the right. But I was determined not to risk my life by foolishly rushing in between speeding vehicles. So I stood there patiently. There was a break in the traffic to my right, but not to my left. Suddenly, I saw a huge vehicle approaching me and then slowing down. It stopped about thirty feet to my left. It was the biggest, most intimidating black Hummer I had ever seen. Adding to the intimidation was its tinted windows so that I couldn't see the driver. And he was waiting patiently to protect me from oncoming traffic so that I could cross safely. The vehicle looked like Darth Vader on steroids and made me burst out with laughter.

THE ONCE WRATH-FILLED LAW BECOMES OUR FRIEND. IN JESUS, WE CAN MAKE THE CROSSING SAFELY.

The great vehicle of Eternal Justice grinds to a halt for sinners because of the cross. The once wrath-filled Law becomes our friend. In Jesus, we can make the crossing safely.

CHAPTER Seven

THE PARTY IS OVER

Through the wonderful cross of Christ, God has given us a new song. While the world rejoices in the pleasures of sin, we sing for joy that God has delivered us from death. There is no comparison to what we have in Christ. Thanks be to God for His indescribable gift!

> Then Moses and the children of Israel sang this song to the LORD, and spoke, saying:
> "I will sing to the LORD,
> For He has triumphed gloriously!
> The horse and its rider
> He has thrown into the sea!" (Exodus 15:1)

The pale horse that carried Death upon its back was thrown into the sea. In Christ, God's right hand became glorious in power and dashed the enemy in pieces. After seeing the cross and the triumph of the resurrection, how can we not say, "Who is like You, O LORD, among the gods? Who is like You, glorious in holiness, fearful in praises, doing wonders?" (Exodus 15:11).

But Israel's song and dance didn't last long. Immediately after the Red Sea experience, something sobering happened:

So Moses brought Israel from the Red Sea; then they went out into the Wilderness of Shur. And they went three days in the wilderness and found no water. Now when they came to Marah, they could not drink the waters of Marah, for they were bitter. Therefore the name of it was called Marah. And the people complained against Moses, saying, "What shall we drink?" (Exodus 15:22–24)

How everything changes when we see the cross. We fall to our knees, broken at such love. God's amazing grace reaches into our very soul and we are born again. In Christ, we are given a new heart with new desires, and God puts a new song on our lips. We see Him who is invisible, are seated in heavenly places, and taste the Bread of Heaven. But we suddenly come down to earth with a thud. We have to come down from the Mount of Transfiguration. This is because have to live in a fallen world until our body of corruption is changed. Like Israel, we pass through the Red Sea of deliverance, but after the miracle of conversion, we find we are in a dry and barren wilderness and often the only water we can find is bitter.

HOW EVERYTHING CHANGES WHEN WE SEE THE CROSS. WE FALL TO OUR KNEES, BROKEN AT SUCH LOVE.

Drinking the water of bitterness is to enter a dark cave that has danger signs at the entrance. To dig into memories of past wrongs done to us is to chip away at the walls until we cause a cave-in that will trap us in a place that will eventually run out of oxygen. Never do it. Forget past wrongs. Stay out of that dark cave no matter how safe the devil tells you it is. It is a

110

trap. Believe the warning signs. If you enter, you will want to take others with you. Look at the warning Scripture gives us:

> Pursue peace with all people, and holiness, without which no one will see the Lord: looking carefully lest anyone fall short of the grace of God; *lest any root of bitterness springing up cause trouble, and by this many become defiled* ... (Hebrews 12:14,15)

If someone has wronged you, pursue peace by forgiving them, *because you have tasted God's grace*. He has forgiven you. Don't fall short of that grace, because if you lack it and let bitterness into your heart, you are going to cause trouble. And if you have pulled other Christians into the cave, you will give the enemy a victory and many will become defiled. Many a local church has crumbled because someone said that the pastor had wronged him and secretly passed on the poison to their church members. In time, the atmosphere is sucked of oxygen and the church dies.

But when Moses cried out to the LORD about the bitter waters, "the LORD showed him a tree. When he cast it into the waters, the waters were made sweet" (Exodus 15:25).

Look at what the apostles said when they were arrested and put on trial for preaching the gospel:

> But Peter and the other apostles answered and said: "We ought to obey God rather than men. The God of our fathers raised up Jesus whom you murdered by hanging on a tree. Him God has exalted to His right hand to be Prince and Savior, to give repentance to Israel and forgiveness of sins. And we are His witnesses to these things, and so also is the Holy Spirit whom God has given to those who obey Him." (Acts 5:29–32)

The word "tree" in Scripture is synonymous with the cross, as Jesus was nailed to a wooden cross. When the poison of bitterness tempts you to drink its defiling waters, throw the cross into the waters. Remember the crucified Savior suffered for you so that you could taste of God's grace and extend that grace toward others. To do that is to obey the warning sign and stay away. We do this because we want to "diligently heed the voice of the LORD your God and do what is right in His sight, give ear to His commandments and keep all His statutes" (Exodus 15:26), and in doing so we will save ourselves and others great grief.

> Then they [the Israelites] came to Elim, where there were twelve wells of water and seventy palm trees; so they camped there by the waters. (Exodus 15:27)

Here is how a Christians lives. He shelters in Christ from the heat of God's wrath, and at the same time drinks from the wells of salvation.

THE WISDOM OF CYNICISM

When I wanted to buy a shirt online, I found exactly what I wanted. It looked great. It's not easy to find shirts for short people. It's also not easy to find an appropriate color—not too bright and not too dull. But what I had found was absolutely perfect. It was made for Comfort.

Being a little cynical, I went to the customer reviews and clicked on the one-star reviews. Here are three of them:

> What I received today is truly disgusting. A used, stained, cologne drenched men's shirt.

> What is wrong with this shirt?! It has a horrible smell that doesn't go away no matter how many times you

wash it or how long you soak it in detergent! It is absolutely disgusting!

Where to begin? Let's start with the SMELL. These shirts smell like sewage. I noticed an odor when I first opened the package and I immediately washed these shirts. It simply will not wash out.

Here is my problem in reading these complaints. I believe the biblical testimony of the human heart, that it is desperately wicked (see Jeremiah 17:9). We can see the truth of this wickedness in daily headlines, with corruption in every area of society. And as our godless society becomes more godless, the less trust there is among people. We naturally become cynical. There was a time when you could buy a house or a car in minutes by just signing one or two forms. Nowadays, it takes hours of reading and signing, because few trust the human heart. So here's my dilemma with my prospective shirt. Were these *genuine* complaints about a crooked shirt company? Or were they fake complaints, placed there by a crooked competing shirt company that wanted to put them out of business?

And so as godly people we fully trust only God, who Himself tells us where to put our trust:

Thus says the LORD:
"Cursed is the man who trusts in man
And makes flesh his strength,
Whose heart departs from the LORD.
For he shall be like a shrub in the desert,
And shall not see when good comes,
But shall inhabit the parched places in the wilderness,
In a salt land which is not inhabited.

"Blessed is the man who trusts in the LORD,
And whose hope is the LORD.
For he shall be like a tree planted by the waters,
Which spreads out its roots by the river,
And will not fear when heat comes;
But its leaf will be green,
And will not be anxious in the year of drought,
Nor will cease from yielding fruit." (Jeremiah 17:5–8)

Exodus chapters 16 and 17 show us that the children of Israel *didn't* trust God. Even though they had seen His mighty power, they didn't have faith in Him to provide for their daily needs. And there was a reason for that.

THE JETSONS

We are living in the excitement of the Jetsons' age, and the irony is that this generation doesn't even know it. *The Jetsons* was a 1960's TV program about a space-age family who lived in a futuristic dwelling in the sky, got around in flying cars and jetpacks, communicated long-distance by video chat, and had a robot maid to take care of anything not handled by countless automated devices—the ultimate "smart" home.

For this generation, there's no real sense of excitement with modern technology, because they take it for granted that this is the way things have always been. But when I leave my home and shut my garage door from a distance with a remote control, when I change the channel on the TV without getting up, when I speak to my iPhone or am guided by GPS, I'm in awe. When I write a book in two months that years ago would have taken me six months to research and tap out on an archaic typewriter, I'm delirious with excitement—*because I know where we have come from and therefore appreciate where we have come to.*

So it is with the coming Kingdom. I have lived long enough on this tragic, fallen earth to experience pain, to see anguish, and to feel the futility of hopelessness—and to appreciate with delirious excitement what God has done for us and the glorious promises He has given us in Christ. Remembering the past and looking forward to the future is what sustains me in the present.

Yet when trials came to the children of Israel, they forgot what God had just done for them—and what He promised to do. Those two things should have sustained them, but they didn't.

They had journeyed for about six weeks when "the whole congregation of the children of Israel complained against Moses and Aaron in the wilderness. And the children of Israel said to them, 'Oh, that we had died by the hand of the LORD in the land of Egypt, when we sat by the pots of meat and when we ate bread to the full! For you have brought us out into this wilderness to kill this whole assembly with hunger'" (Exodus 16:3). God kindly showered manna from Heaven and provided quail for them to eat:

> And the LORD spoke to Moses, saying, "I have heard the complaints of the children of Israel. Speak to them, saying, 'At twilight you shall eat meat, and in the morning you shall be filled with bread. And you shall know that I am the LORD your God.'" (Exodus 16:11,12)

Then they complained to Moses about being thirsty:

> Then all the congregation of the children of Israel set out on their journey from the Wilderness of Sin, according to the commandment of the LORD, and camped in Rephidim; but there was no water for the people to

115

drink. Therefore the people contended with Moses, and said, "Give us water, that we may drink."

So Moses said to them, "Why do you contend with me? Why do you tempt the LORD?"

And the people thirsted there for water, and the people complained against Moses, and said, "Why is it you have brought us up out of Egypt, to kill us and our children and our livestock with thirst?" (Exodus 17:1–3)

Let me ask you a searching question: Are you tempted to sympathize with the children of Israel? They were very thirsty. So were their kids and cattle. They were so thirsty they thought that they might die in the wilderness. In a sense, their complaint was understandable. But notice the words "according to the commandment of the LORD." They were in the wilderness *because that's where God wanted them to be.* He directed them to go there, determined how long they would stay, and told them when to move on.

Instead of whining to Moses, they should have looked to the heavens and said something like, "LORD, You delivered us from our enemies! You miraculously opened the Red Sea! *There is none like You.* We now trust You to supply our needs and the needs of our precious loved ones..." Instead, they ignored the LORD and murmured against Moses. As far as they were concerned, God wasn't worth trusting.

When trials come our way, how easy it is to forget the deliverance of the cross. The problems can be both real and painful. But the question is, *how do we react in our darkest times?* How easy it is to set aside the exceedingly great and precious promises we have in Christ when things suddenly turn bad.

Despite the many miracles they had seen, the children of Israel *didn't* trust God. They murmured, complained, and whined, and then they contended with Moses. But look again at verse 3. This was no ordinary whining:

> And the people thirsted there for water, and the people complained against Moses, and said, "Why is it you have brought us up out of Egypt, to kill us and our children and our livestock with thirst?"
>
> So Moses cried out to the LORD, saying, "What shall I do with this people? They are almost ready to stone me!" (Exodus 17:3,4)

They thought that *Moses* had taken them into the wilderness, when *God* had put them there. Then they accused Moses of trying to kill them. They so forgot their Creator that they blamed Moses for their predicament and were ready to murder him.

Unbelief produces fear and with fear comes suspicion and disunity. We blame others when we forget that God often leads us into the wilderness, and when that happens we begin to whine.

THEY THOUGHT THAT MOSES HAD TAKEN THEM INTO THE WILDERNESS, WHEN *GOD* HAD PUT THEM THERE.

I love my dog. However, Sam has always had a habit of whining. Whenever he didn't get his own way, he would send out the most annoying low frequency sound through his nostrils. It had the same effect as the sound of a dentist drill. He did it many times a day, sometimes for no reason. But one day I remembered that dogs have a keen sense of smell, up to 100,000 times better than a human. I also remembered that most dogs lift up their front lip in disgust at salt-and-vinegar potato chips. They do the same with a lemon.

So I grabbed a fresh-smelling lemon off our lemon tree, cut off the top, and brought it close to Sam's sensitive whining nose. Sure enough, it was his kryptonite. He backed off like a politician backs off from a searching question. And so we have a fresh lemon regularly waiting on our kitchen counter. Whenever Sam even thinks of murmuring, we pick up the lemon, and he backs off with quivering lips and sits in golden silence like a good dog.

The Scriptures give us insight into the whining hearts of the children of Israel:

> But they sinned even more against Him
> By rebelling against the Most High in the wilderness.
> And they tested God in their heart
> By asking for the food of their fancy.
> Yes, they spoke against God:
> They said, "Can God prepare a table in the wilderness?
> Behold, He struck the rock,
> So that the waters gushed out,
> And the streams overflowed.
> Can He give bread also?
> Can He provide meat for His people?" (Psalm 78:17–20)

THE LEMON

When we seriously consider the power of God, we set sail on the ocean of possibility. If the Lord is the Creator of everything in this universe, *nothing* is impossible for Him. But Israel didn't consider this, and instead rebelled against the Most High. They tested Him in their hearts and asked whether or not God had the ability to provide for them in the wilderness.

Unbelief is birthed because of thoughtlessness—and there is nothing as thoughtless as atheism. It is a dark and hopeless room in which the window to trust in God is nailed shut. When physicist Stephen Hawking died at the age of seventy-six, he apparently died as a hopeless atheist. He told the *Guardian* in 2011 that he often thought of death. He said,

I have lived with the prospect of an early death for the last 49 years. I'm not afraid of death, but I'm in no hurry to die. I have so much I want to do first.[15]

WHEN WE SERIOUSLY CONSIDER THE POWER OF GOD, WE SET SAIL ON THE OCEAN OF POSSIBILITY.

He continued,

I regard the brain as a computer which will stop working when its components fail. There is no heaven or afterlife for broken down computers; that is a fairy story for people afraid of the dark.[16]

The insanity of unbelief that comes with the thoughtlessness of atheism is rooted in pride:

The wicked in his proud countenance does not seek
God;
God is in none of his thoughts...
He has said in his heart,
"God has forgotten;
He hides His face;
He will never see." (Psalm 10:4,11)

The atheist believes that unbelief rids him of the problem of moral accountability to God and the burden of guilt. He believes that it therefore gives him license to sin. And behind a heart of unbelief lies nothing but a love for the pleasures of sin. Men love darkness rather than light, because their deeds are evil (John 3:19).

But the air in which they think they find freedom will eventually choke them to death and drag them to Hell—where they will become reluctant believers.

Upon Hawking's untimely death, *Time* magazine wrote:

> Hawking invoked the name of God in his seminal book *A Brief History of Time*, writing that if physicists could find a "theory of everything"—that is, a cohesive explanation for how the universe works—they would glimpse "the mind of God."[17]
>
> But in later interviews and writings, such as 2010's *The Grand Design*, which he co-wrote with American theoretical physicist Leonard Mlodinow, Hawking clarified that he wasn't referring to a creator in the traditional sense.
>
> "Spontaneous creation is the reason there is something rather than nothing, why the universe exists, why we exist," he wrote in *The Grand Design*. "It is not necessary to invoke God to light the blue touch paper and set the universe going."[18]

As the famous atheist Richard Dawkins is drawing nearer to the end of his life, he was asked how he viewed his upcoming death:

> At the close of our conversation, I asked Dawkins how he viewed the prospect of death. "I find the idea of eternity and infinity frightening... Death is a general anesthetic." And what of his posthumous reputation? "I do derive great comfort from the thought that I've written quite a number of books and they're very widely read and I hope that they will go on being read. I depart from

Woody Allen's remark: 'I don't want to live on in my works, I want to live on in my apartment.'"[19]

Here is the entire impetus and philosophy of atheism in just one verse:

"The mind of the flesh [with its sinful pursuits] is actively hostile to God. It does not submit itself to God's law, since it cannot..." (Romans 8:7, AMP)

Atheism is to believe the scientific impossibility that nothing created everything. Such convictions are delusional and leave those who embrace lack of faith in God in the same predicament as the unfaithful children of Israel. They put themselves under the just wrath of God:

Therefore the LORD heard this and was furious;
So a fire was kindled against Jacob,
And anger also came up against Israel,
Because they did not believe in God,
And did not trust in His salvation.
Yet He had commanded the clouds above,
And opened the doors of heaven,
Had rained down manna on them to eat,
And given them of the bread of heaven.
Men ate angels' food;
He sent them food to the full.
... So they ate and were well filled,
For He gave them their own desire.
They were not deprived of their craving;
But while their food was still in their mouths,
The wrath of God came against them,
And slew the stoutest of them,
And struck down the choice men of Israel.
(Psalm 78:21–25, 29–31)

These frightening verses should be a lemon to our whining nose. They should make us back off from unbelief and instead trust God's promises. Unbelief in the hearts of the children of Israel caused them to provoke, grieve, tempt, and limit God, all because they forgot His power and that He had graciously redeemed them from the hand of the enemy:

MOST IN THIS WORLD HAVE NO IDEA THAT IT WAS THE ROD OF THE LAW THAT CONDEMNED THEM TO DEATH.

> How often they provoked Him in
> the wilderness,
> And grieved Him in the desert!
> Yes, again and again they tempted
> God,
> And limited the Holy One of Israel.
> They did not remember His power:
> The day when He redeemed them from the enemy.
> (Psalm 78:40–42)

THE SAFEGUARD AGAINST UNBELIEF

Scripture then gives us the antidote to the fatal disease of unbelief. The LORD told Moses to take in his hand the rod that he used to turn the river into blood. When he struck the river with it, it meant that the waters would no longer give life to the Egyptians.

Most in this world have no idea that it was the rod of the Law that condemned them to death. It proclaimed the death sentence to all of humanity. "The soul who sins shall die" (Ezekiel 18:20), because "sin" is transgression of the Law (see 1 John 3:4).

Moses was to take that rod and strike a rock. God said, "*Behold, I will stand before you there on the rock* in Horeb;

and you shall strike the rock, and water will come out of it, that the people may drink" (Exodus 17:6).

God Himself would be on the rock that was struck by Moses. When Jesus was struck for our sins by the rod of Eternal Justice, God was in Christ bringing the world back to Himself (see 2 Corinthians 5:19).

The book of Numbers gives us further insight into this incident:

> "Take the rod; you and your brother Aaron gather the congregation together. Speak to the rock before their eyes, and it will yield its water; thus you shall bring water for them out of the rock, and give drink to the congregation and their animals." So Moses took the rod from before the LORD as He commanded him.
>
> And Moses and Aaron gathered the assembly together before the rock; and he said to them, "Hear now, you rebels! Must we bring water for you out of this rock?" Then Moses lifted his hand and struck the rock twice with his rod; and water came out abundantly, and the congregation and their animals drank.
>
> Then the LORD spoke to Moses and Aaron, "Because you did not believe Me, to hallow Me in the eyes of the children of Israel, therefore you shall not bring this assembly into the land which I have given them." (Numbers 20:8–12)

Scripture tells us that Jesus was the Rock that was struck for us, and from Him flows living water:

> Moreover, brethren, I do not want you to be unaware that all our fathers were under the cloud, all passed through the sea, all were baptized into Moses in the cloud and in the sea, all ate the same spiritual food, and

all drank the same spiritual drink. *For they drank of that spiritual Rock that followed them, and that Rock was Christ.* But with most of them God was not well pleased, for their bodies were scattered in the wilderness. (1 Corinthians 10:1–5)

On the last day, that great day of the feast, Jesus stood and cried out, saying, "If anyone thirsts, let him come to Me and drink. He who believes in Me, as the Scripture has said, out of his heart will flow rivers of living water." (John 7:37,38)

And all these things are recorded as examples for us:

Now these things became our examples, to the intent that we should not lust after evil things as they also lusted. *And do not become idolaters as were some of them.* As it is written, "The people sat down to eat and drink, and rose up to play." Nor let us commit sexual immorality, as some of them did, and in one day twenty-three thousand fell; nor let us tempt Christ, as some of them also tempted, and were destroyed by serpents; nor complain, as some of them also complained, and were destroyed by the destroyer. Now all these things happened to them as examples, and they were written for our admonition, upon whom the ends of the ages have come. (1 Corinthians 10:6–11)

Unbelief is the result of idolatry, just as a right view of God's character and nature produces truth. But when idolatry perverts that understanding and reduces the character of God, unbelief is the result. It shrinks Almighty God to an impotent and dumb idol.

Moses then angered God because he struck the rock twice. Once was enough:

For Christ also suffered *once* for sins, the just for the unjust, that He might bring us to God, being put to death in the flesh but made alive by the Spirit. (1 Peter 3:18)

Moses puts salvation beyond our grasp. It leaves us without hope of securing it by our own works, so that our only avenue is to plead for mercy, of which God is rich. The suffering death of Jesus was enough and secured salvation to all who trust in Him. It was finished on the cross. There's no need for Him to be offered again. There is no need for the Rock to be struck twice.

Moses can't take us into the Promised Land. He leads us as a tutor to Jesus, and Jesus takes us by the hand.

A MOMENT OF INTROSPECTION

Before we call fire from Heaven on the rebellious children of Israel and foolish atheists for their unbelief, let's take this sin of unbelief a little further. Do we share the gospel with strangers? If we don't, could it be because of the sin of unbelief? Are we fearful because we aren't trusting Him to lead us and speak through us?

Listen to Charles Spurgeon speak to the issue of the fearful Christian:

If you are of a nervous temperament and of retiring disposition, take care that you do not too much indulge this trembling propensity, lest you should be useless to the church. Seek in the name of him who was not ashamed of you to do some little violence to your feelings, and tell to others what Christ has told to you. If thou canst not speak with trumpet tongue, use the still small voice. If the pulpit must not be thy tribune, if the

125

press may not carry on its wings thy words, yet say with Peter and John, "Silver and gold have I none; but such as I have give I thee."

By Sychar's well talk to the Samaritan woman, if thou canst not on the mountain preach a sermon; utter the praises of Jesus in the house, if not in the temple; in the field, if not upon the exchange; in the midst of thine own household, if thou canst not in the midst of the great family of man. From the hidden springs within let sweetly flowing rivulets of testimony flow forth, giving drink to every passer-by. Hide not thy talent; trade with it; and thou shalt bring in good interest to thy Lord and Master. To speak for God will be refreshing to ourselves, cheering to saints, useful to sinners, and honoring to the Saviour.[20]

CHAPTER Eight

THE BATTLE
OF MORALITY

We are certainly living in difficult times. There were periods in recent history where it did look like there was a chance that we could hold back the flood of immorality. Back in the 1980s the church became a political force with which the world had to reckon. But as its message changed and a lawless gospel opened wide the straight gate, the church was flooded with false converts.

In 2019, Barna Research revealed that the latest generation of professed Christians lacks theological depth:

> Almost all practicing Christians believe that part of their faith means being a witness about Jesus (ranging from 95% to 97% among all generational groups), and that the best thing that could ever happen to someone is for them to know Jesus (94% to 97%). Millennials in particular feel equipped to share their faith with others. For instance, almost three-quarters say they know how to respond when someone raises questions about faith (73%), and that they are gifted at sharing their faith with other people (73%). This is higher than any other generational group: Gen X (66%), Boomers (59%) and Elders (56%).

Despite this, many Millennials are unsure about the actual practice of evangelism. Almost half of Millennials (47%) agree at least somewhat that it is wrong to share one's personal beliefs with someone of a different faith in hopes that they will one day share the same faith. This is compared to a little over one-quarter of Gen X (27%), and one in five Boomers (19%) and Elders (20%).[21]

How could anyone who has been born again think that it's wrong to save people from Hell? The only logical conclusion is that they think the One they profess to love and follow was wrong when He said He was the only way to the Father (see John 14:6), and that He is to be ignored when He said to "go into *all* the world and preach the gospel to every creature" (Mark 16:15). All who are not trusting in the mercy of God in Christ are still in their sins, and we must plead with them to come to the cross. As we have seen, this can be done without offense if Moses precedes Jesus.

As the light of the gospel has become less visible, our ability to be salt in a morally rotting society has been greatly reduced, and abortion, homosexuality, fornication, adultery, pornography, and blasphemy have become socially acceptable. The church has lost its way as the guiding light in the dark storm, and the tragic consequence is that society has become morally shipwrecked.

But all is not lost. God can turn disaster into victory. Moses and his rod can instruct us on how we can rescue a dying generation:

> Now Amalek came and fought with Israel in Rephidim. And Moses said to Joshua, "Choose us some men and go out, fight with Amalek. Tomorrow I will stand on

the top of the hill with the rod of God in my hand." So Joshua did as Moses said to him, and fought with Amalek. And Moses, Aaron, and Hur went up to the top of the hill. And so it was, when Moses held up his hand, that Israel prevailed; and when he let down his hand, Amalek prevailed. But Moses' hands became heavy; so they took a stone and put it under him, and he sat on it. And Aaron and Hur supported his hands, one on one side, and the other on the other side; and his hands were steady until the going down of the sun. So Joshua defeated Amalek and his people with the edge of the sword.

Then the LORD said to Moses, "Write this for a memorial in the book and recount it in the hearing of Joshua, that I will utterly blot out the remembrance of Amalek from under heaven." And Moses built an altar and called its name, The-LORD-Is-My-Banner; for he said, "Because the LORD has sworn: the LORD will have war with Amalek from generation to generation." (Exodus 17:8–16)

We are at war. Behind moral degeneration is a subtle enemy—the god of this world who blinds the minds of the unsaved (see 2 Corinthians 4:3,4). And he knows that his defeat comes about when we stand on a hill and uphold the rod of Moses.

I hope you are grasping the gravity of what God has given us in His Law. We have a very real enemy who hates this principle, and the blindness to the biblical use of the Law was evidenced in the testimony someone sent me:

I was a 26-year-old man or so when you came to Dallas First Assembly of God. I'm sure you remember—Bob Rogers was our pastor. I love that he endorsed your book *Hell's Best Kept Secret*. I purchased the paperback and *My Friends Are Dying* [retitled *Out of the Comfort Zone*] when you visited back in the '90s, and read them intently. Even after that, I guess I still needed to really think about how the Law brings us to a state of helplessness so that we run to the cross in order to escape God's wrath. Well, it took many years for me to understand. I was just slow on the uptake, I guess. Through the next 20+ or so years I struggled in how to share my faith. It was awkward. I would ask people, "Has anybody ever explained the gospel of Jesus Christ to you?" I had a few good conversations, but in my naivety I didn't realize that I was trying to share the good news without helping the person I was talking to first understand how they had broken God's Law—in order to get their conscience to agree with what it already knew. I was frustrated because I was only partially successful (in my mind), but also didn't realize that I was getting everything backwards.

Then I came across your YouTube channel in early 2018 and began watching. I started to see the correct model for evangelism and, like a light bulb in my heart, it switched on. My conscience had always agreed that I had broken His Law, and even when you came to Dallas First Assembly of God, I remember being broken inside. But this time, I realized that I was that wounded dog who had found care and nursing back to health and that now I had the correct tools for helping other "wounded dogs" find God's forgiveness and healing for the soul.

I had always felt a burden for the lost, but evangelism was so awkward—because I hadn't learned the correct way to talk to folks. After seeing many of your one-on-ones and videos at Huntington Beach, I started to hear myself saying, like Kirk Cameron says in the plug for the School of Biblical Evangelism, "I can do that!" I ordered my first batch of celebrity million dollar bills [tracts, available at livingwaters.com] and started handing them out and talking to folks everywhere I went— the office, the grocery store, the home improvement store...everywhere. I also found it much easier to break the ice with people, and have become more gregarious and friendly, because I do truly care about the plight of mankind. I was walking people through the Law and then the gospel—the model that you have used for decades. I also signed up for the School of Biblical Evangelism and began to study even more. I memorized Scripture and I used that Scripture when I talked with folks. I finally felt like I was helping build God's kingdom, the right way. And, to God be the glory, I was finally evangelizing, finally putting my love for people into action. I am equipped and with my "feet shod with the gospel of peace," am "redeeming the time for the days are evil." —Your fellow co-laborer in Christ

May God raise up these faithful men and women who will stand on the mountaintop and uphold Moses with the rod of God in his hand. It is that which will bring victory in the battle against abortion. It is the Law in the hand of the Spirit that will overcome adultery, blasphemy, murder, hatred, covetousness, idolatry, fornication, and every other sin that is an offense to God.

Without that moral compass sinners have no fear of God, and they will therefore embrace sin's pleasures with reckless abandon. Why should sinners flee from wrath if the church refuses to tell them that there is wrath to come? We evangelize biblically when we do what Jesus did as He lifted up the Law on a mountaintop. In the Sermon on the Mount, He said,

> "For assuredly, I say to you, till heaven and earth pass away, one jot or one tittle will by no means pass from the law till all is fulfilled. Whoever therefore breaks one of the least of these commandments, and teaches men so, shall be called least in the kingdom of heaven; but whoever does and teaches them, he shall be called great in the kingdom of heaven. For I say to you, that unless your righteousness exceeds the righteousness of the scribes and Pharisees, you will by no means enter the kingdom of heaven." (Matthew 5:18–20)

WE EVANGELIZE BIBLICALLY WHEN WE DO WHAT JESUS DID AS HE LIFTED UP THE LAW ON A MOUNTAINTOP.

Jesus opened up the spiritual nature of the Law and showed that the outward precepts of religion leave us in our sins, because God requires truth in the inward parts:

> "You have heard that it was said to those of old, 'You shall not murder, and whoever murders will be in danger of the judgment.' But I say to you that whoever is angry with his brother without a cause shall be in danger of the judgment. And whoever says to his brother, 'Raca!' shall be in danger of the council. But whoever says, 'You fool!' shall be in danger of hell fire." (Matthew 5:21,22)

Never hesitate to expound that same Law. Never fear to lovingly, gently, and uncompromisingly lift it high by opening up its meaning to bring light to sinners. When the world hears the thunder of Sinai, the conscience bears witness that every precept is right, just, holy, and good. Watch as Jesus raised the arms of Moses:

> "You have heard that it was said to those of old, 'You shall not commit adultery.' But I say to you that whoever looks at a woman to lust for her has already committed adultery with her in his heart. If your right eye causes you to sin, pluck it out and cast it from you; for it is more profitable for you that one of your members perish, than for your whole body to be cast into hell. And if your right hand causes you to sin, cut it off and cast it from you; for it is more profitable for you that one of your members perish, than for your whole body to be cast into hell." (Matthew 5:27–30)

How can sinners not tremble to hear such words! There is no seeking of shelter if there is no storm predicted. God has taken the time to record how to predict the storm:

> But we know that the law is good if one uses it lawfully, knowing this: that the law is not made for a righteous person, but for the lawless and insubordinate, for the ungodly and for sinners, for the unholy and profane, for murderers of fathers and murderers of mothers, for manslayers, for fornicators, for sodomites, for kidnappers, for liars, for perjurers, and if there is any other thing that is contrary to sound doctrine… (1 Timothy 1:8–10)

Build a stone altar to this teaching. Don't let generations of Christians forget how to defeat the enemy. Remember Barna's research:

> Almost half of Millennials (47%) agree at least somewhat that it is wrong to share one's personal beliefs with

someone of a different faith in hopes that they will one day share the same faith.[22]

It is knowledge of the Law that gives us good reason to plead with every Hell-bound sinner—whether they are arrogant atheists, apathetic agnostics, or a lost son or daughter of Adam who is vainly seeking salvation through dead religion.

SPREAD THE LOAD

A great key to any successful endeavor is delegation. Look at the wisdom given to Moses from his father-in-law, Jethro:

> And so it was, on the next day, that Moses sat to judge the people; and the people stood before Moses from morning until evening. So when Moses' father-in-law saw all that he did for the people, he said, "What is this thing that you are doing for the people? Why do you alone sit, and all the people stand before you from morning until evening?"
>
> And Moses said to his father-in-law, "Because the people come to me to inquire of God. When they have a difficulty, they come to me, and I judge between one and another; and I make known the statutes of God and His laws."
>
> So Moses' father-in-law said to him, "The thing that you do is not good. Both you and these people who are with you will surely wear yourselves out. For this thing is too much for you; you are not able to perform it by yourself." (Exodus 18:13–18)

Here is Jethro's wise advice:

> "Listen now to my voice; I will give you counsel, and God will be with you: Stand before God for the people, so that you may bring the difficulties to God. And you

shall teach them the statutes and the laws, and show them the way in which they must walk and the work they must do." (Exodus 18:19,20)

We need Jethros. We need those wise and faithful brethren who will tell the church that limiting the work of Moses is not good. When we teach the statutes of the Law as Jesus did, we are revealing "the way in which they must walk and the work they must do." We exist to reach the lost. We *must* work while it is yet day. We *must* go through Samaria. We *must* warn every man, that we may present every man perfect before a perfect Law on the Day of Wrath.

ISRAEL AT MOUNT SINAI

In the third month after the children of Israel had gone out of the land of Egypt, on the same day, they came to the Wilderness of Sinai. For they had departed from Rephidim, had come to the Wilderness of Sinai, and camped in the wilderness. So Israel camped there before the mountain. (Exodus 19:1,2)

The Scriptures use the words "wilderness of Sinai" when speaking of Mount Sinai. The Law is indeed a barren desert. It cannot give life, but as we have seen it brings us to Him who gives the waters of everlasting life to hopeless sinners. It should therefore never be despised or ignored.

Early in 2019, a popular megachurch pastor said that the moral Law was irrelevant. He said that the Ten Commandments no longer applied and that Christians instead should focus on Jesus' Sermon on the Mount. After quoting Jesus' words, "A new command I give you: Love one another. As I have loved you, so you must love one another" (John 13:34),

Andy Stanley, pastor of North Point Community Church in Georgia, said,

> "Jesus didn't issue his new command [John 13:34] as an additional commandment to the existing list of commands. The early church moved past the old covenant —why haven't we?"

The article on Christian Headlines went on to say,

> Debates over the public display of the Ten Commandments, he said, are unnecessary.
>
> "You've heard the story before: A group of Christians puts up a monument of the Ten Commandments in a public space or on government property," Stanley wrote. "Someone says it violates the separation of church and state. The Christians say taking it down would violate their freedom of speech. There's some back and forth in court and both sides say some not-so-great things about the other. Rinse and repeat."
>
> "But how many times," Stanley asked, "have you seen Christians trying to post the text of the sermon on the mount in a public place? Or the all-encompassing commandment Jesus gave us?"
>
> Stanley quoted John 13:34: "A new command I give you: Love one another. As I have loved you, so you must love one another."
>
> He called it the "one commandment."
>
> "Doesn't have the same ring to it, does it? But if we're going to create a monument to stand as a testament to our faith," Stanley wrote, "shouldn't it at least be a monument of something that actually applies to us?"
>
> Jesus may have been "foreshadowed in the old covenant," Stanley wrote, but "he did not come to extend it."

"He came to fulfill it, put a bow on it, and establish something entirely new," Stanley wrote. "...The author of Hebrews says it best. Jesus was the 'guarantor of a better covenant' (Hebrews 7:22). Later he writes, 'the new covenant is established on better promises.'"[23]

In the Sermon on the Mount, Jesus is exalting the Law and making it honorable (see Isaiah 42:21). The psalmist said, "Oh, how I love Your law! It is my meditation all the day" (Psalm 119:97). The apostle Paul said, "I delight in the law of God according to the inward man" (Romans 7:22). If we want to see people come to Christ we must not pull down the uplifted hands of Moses. If we long for sinners to listen to Jesus, they must first listen to Moses. Jesus said, "If they do not hear Moses and the prophets, neither will they be persuaded though one rise from the dead" (Luke 16:31).

IF WE LONG FOR SINNERS TO LISTEN TO JESUS, THEY MUST FIRST LISTEN TO MOSES.

It is a tragic mistake to forsake the Law, because it leaves a nation without the knowledge of sin, and it will consequentially embrace idolatry and lose the fear of God. To forsake the Law is to leave sinners in moral darkness, "For the commandment is a lamp, and the law a light" (Proverbs 6:23). We should rather put it between the frontlets of the eyes of the world so that they are reminded of their Creator's demands.

God loves justice. He loves truth and righteousness, and all these are embodied in His Law. In Exodus we see that He prepares Israel for a big event. *Really* big. Monumental, in fact. He is going to give them the Ten Commandments. Look at how they are to get ready:

And the LORD said to Moses, "Behold, I come to you in the thick cloud, that the people may hear when I speak with you, and believe you forever."

So Moses told the words of the people to the LORD.

Then the LORD said to Moses, "Go to the people and consecrate them today and tomorrow, and let them wash their clothes. And let them be ready for the third day. For on the third day the LORD will come down upon Mount Sinai in the sight of all the people. You shall set bounds for the people all around, saying, 'Take heed to yourselves that you do not go up to the mountain or touch its base. Whoever touches the mountain shall surely be put to death. Not a hand shall touch him, but he shall surely be stoned or shot with an arrow; whether man or beast, he shall not live.' When the trumpet sounds long, they shall come near the mountain."

So Moses went down from the mountain to the people and sanctified the people, and they washed their clothes. And he said to the people, "Be ready for the third day; do not come near your wives." (Exodus 19:9–15)

When a heinous criminal stands in the dock, the judge will soberly read the law to him so that his transgression becomes clear. God was about to do that to Israel. This was a most sober moment. The men were told not to go indulge in sex. It was like a father saying to his son, "Put away your toys for a moment, son, and come here. I want to speak to you about something *very* serious." And the Law is deadly serious. It is the basis for our death sentence.

This was no earthly judge. This One was robed in thick cloud. If He was not covered, those who looked upon His holiness would instantly die. He is a consuming fire, and He shines above the brightness of the sun.

THE HORRIBLE SIGHT

I was horrified as I looked ahead on the road in front of me. I could see the tragic sight of a rather large dead dog. It had obviously been hit by a car and its strewn body was left lying, terribly mangled, in the middle of the busy road. Even from a distance, I could see that it was a big animal—perhaps a German Shepherd. The dog's characteristic pointed ears and head were still recognizable even though its body was mangled.

As I got closer I felt physically sick at the sight. Suddenly, I felt stupid. It was just an old coat that had perhaps fallen off a homeless person's bike.

A fertile imagination is normally a great blessing. We can be entertained by familiar shapes in clouds, can imagine an invention, imagine a new house, or imagine what it would be like to win a gold medal at the Olympics. The human imagination can spark a lifelong obsession to achieve fame and fortune. It can be a wonderful and motivating fire in the soul that gives our lives substance and meaning. Albert Einstein said, "Imagination is more important than knowledge. For knowledge is limited, whereas imagination embraces the entire world, stimulating progress, giving birth to evolution."[24]

But like many virtuous things in this life, the imagination can be perverted. We can imagine adultery, murder, and fornication. Lust is fired up by the imagination. It puts unlawful images into our sin-loving mind. God judged Noah's generation because the imagination of their heart was continually evil:

> And God saw that the wickedness of man was great in the earth, and that every imagination of the thoughts of his heart was only evil continually. (Genesis 6:5, KJV)

The sin of idolatry has its foundation in the human imagination. We create an *image* of what we think God is like. And this was the root of Israel's problem. They limited God to the confines of their imagination when He has no limits, and He was about to hit those limits out of the ballpark:

> Then it came to pass on the third day, in the morning, that there were thunderings and lightnings, and a thick cloud on the mountain; and the sound of the trumpet was very loud, so that all the people who were in the camp trembled. And Moses brought the people out of the camp to meet with God, and they stood at the foot of the mountain. Now Mount Sinai was completely in smoke, because the LORD descended upon it in fire. Its smoke ascended like the smoke of a furnace, and the whole mountain quaked greatly. And when the blast of the trumpet sounded long and became louder and louder, Moses spoke, and God answered him by voice. Then the LORD came down upon Mount Sinai, on the top of the mountain. And the LORD called Moses to the top of the mountain, and Moses went up. (Exodus 19:16–20)

The giving of the Law destroyed those imaginary boundaries. He stood before them, in thick cloud, clothed in thunder and lighting, and with a voice that terrified them. May we rightly imagine what they saw, and tremble.

WHAT'S MISSING?

Although I'd been living in the United States for over thirty years, I never drove past a huge globe sculpture in Seal Beach without feeling irritated. The makers had left New Zealand (my home country) off the globe. *How could they?* Was the country too small to bother including it? Don't four million people matter? They are not alone: IKEA issued an apology to New Zealand for selling a map on which the country was omitted.

Scripture tells of how a young David was "left off the map" when God sent Samuel to choose the future king from the seven sons of Jesse:

> So it was, when they came, that he looked at Eliab and said, "Surely the Lord's anointed is before Him!"
>
> But the LORD said to Samuel, "Do not look at his appearance or at his physical stature, because I have refused him. For the LORD does not see as man sees; for man looks at the outward appearance, but the LORD looks at the heart."
>
> So Jesse called Abinadab, and made him pass before Samuel. And he said, "Neither has the LORD chosen this one." Then Jesse made Shammah pass by. And he said, "Neither has the LORD chosen this one." Thus Jesse made seven of his sons pass before Samuel. And Samuel said to Jesse, "The LORD has not chosen these." And Samuel said to Jesse, "Are all the young men here?" Then he said, "There remains yet the youngest, and there he is, keeping the sheep."
>
> And Samuel said to Jesse, "Send and bring him. For we will not sit down till he comes here." So he sent and brought him in. Now he was ruddy, with bright eyes, and good-looking. And the LORD said, "Arise, anoint him; for this is the one!" Then Samuel took the horn of oil and anointed him in the midst of his brothers; and the Spirit of the LORD came upon David from that day forward. So Samuel arose and went to Ramah. (1 Samuel 16:6–13)

We tend to look at this verse and have a warm fuzzy feeling when we see that God goes for the underdog. He chooses the nobodies with nothing. He doesn't see as man sees; He looks upon the heart. But we tend to settle with that thought. But the Bible says that *nothing* is hidden from His omniscient eyes. He sees *everything*. All at once.

Let's break that down a little. God not only knows me by name, He knows every hair on my head. He sees every hair from every angle. He sees the atoms that make up each follicle. Then He sees *within* every proton, electron, and neutron that make up each atom. He is intimately familiar with each one from every angle, because He fashioned each one, from nothing.

THERE IS NO ARGUMENT ABOUT THE EXISTENCE OF GOD, BECAUSE THE HEAVENS DECLARE IT CLEARLY.

On July 4, 1776, when the newly formed states of America were united, the Declaration of Independence *declared* independence. It was a bold statement. There was no room for negotiation.

The Bible says that "the heavens *declare* the glory of God" (Psalm 19:1). The heavens make the boldest of statements. There is no argument about the existence of God, because the heavens declare it clearly. And every atheist who looks toward the heavens sees that declaration and is without excuse (see Romans 1:20).

There are times when I look at the heavens that my breath is taken away in awe and I'm reduced to tear-filled eyes—not because of its beauty, but because of the power of God who created that incredible beauty. While we will never (in this life) fully comprehend His power—from the life of an ant to the vastness of the universe—we can catch a tiny glimpse of it by looking to the heavens and seeing His glory.

But it is even more important for us to also catch a glimpse of His holiness, because that is what will bring us to the cross, and it's what will keep us there.

CHAPTER Nine

CLIMAX OF THE AGES

With the people gathered at the base of Mount Sinai, then came the moment for which all of Israel had been waiting. What would the Creator say? What was on His mind?

"I am the LORD your God, who brought you out of the land of Egypt, out of the house of bondage." (Exodus 20:2)

The Creator began by formally introducing Himself: I am the LORD your God. The Ultimate Authority and the Creator of all things. He reminded the children of Israel of what He'd done for them in delivering them from Egypt. Then He gave them His moral Law. This wasn't a set of ten rules that had come to His mind, but a manifestation of His divine character. The moral Law tells us who our God is, and that Law is what He esteems:

Righteousness and justice are the foundation of Your throne; mercy and truth go before Your face. (Psalm 89:14)

Clouds and darkness surround Him; righteousness and justice are the foundation of His throne. (Psalm 97:2)

Then He cited the first two Commandments:

"You shall have no other gods before Me.

"You shall not make for yourself a carved image—
any likeness of anything that is in heaven above, or that
is in the earth beneath, or that is in the water under the
earth; you shall not bow down to them nor serve them.
For I, the LORD your God, am a jealous God, visiting
the iniquity of the fathers upon the children to the third
and fourth generations of those who hate Me, but show-
ing mercy to thousands, to those who love Me and keep
My commandments." (Exodus 20:3–6)

In the Roman Catholic catechism, however, number two
is missing. For most Catholics, its mysterious absence isn't
noticed because the Tenth Commandment has been divided
into two:

The First Commandment: I Am the Lord Your God,
You Shall Not Have Other Gods Before Me

The Second Commandment: You Shall Not Take the
Name of the Lord Your God in Vain

The Third Commandment: Remember to Keep Holy
the Lord's Day

The Fourth Commandment: Honor Your Father and
Your Mother

The Fifth Commandment: You Shall Not Kill

The Sixth Commandment: You Shall Not Commit
Adultery

The Seventh Commandment: You Shall Not Steal

The Eighth Commandment: You Shall Not Bear False
Witness Against Your Neighbor

The Ninth Commandment: You Shall Not Covet Your
Neighbor's Wife

The Tenth Commandment: You Shall Not Covet Your
Neighbor's Possessions[25]

This removal of an entire Commandment has left millions of Roman Catholics in the dark as to the sin of bowing down to idols, and if we love these people we have to use the Law to awaken them to their state before God. Our pleading with them doesn't come from hatred, but from the exact opposite.

CLIMBING THE MOUNT

We don't serve sin, but instead live lawfully, as a result of our salvation, not as an effort to earn it. The salvation of those in Christ is already a done deal. It was finished the moment Jesus said on the cross, "It is finished." There's no need to try to climb the holy mount. And those who try will find that if they merely touch it, it will kill them. They want to climb it because they think it will lead them to eternal life, when the opposite is the case.

I was at Huntington Beach, California, parking our car before Scotty and I preached, when I was approached by a man in his late thirties. He said that he wasn't a Christian but that he continually watched the witnessing videos on our YouTube channel.

> THIS REMOVAL OF AN ENTIRE COMMANDMENT HAS LEFT MILLIONS OF ROMAN CATHOLICS IN THE DARK.

After I shared the gospel with him, he said that he was doing his bit to get to Heaven by taking clothes to the poor, something he said he had done a thousand times. Tim was unwittingly seeking justification by the Law. He was trying to climb Mount Sinai.

In the great classic book *Pilgrim's Progress*, a godless man called Legality sent Christian to climb Sinai, telling him that it was the way to Heaven. But Evangelist set him straight:

> And for this you must consider to whom he sent you, and also how unable that person was to deliver you from your burden.
>
> He to whom you were sent for ease, being by name Legality, is the son of the bond-woman which now is, and is in bondage with her children, Gal. 4:21–27, and is, in a mystery, this Mount Sinai, which you have feared will fall on your head. Now if she with her children are in bondage, how can you expect by them to be made free? This Legality, therefore, is not able to set you free from your burden. No man was as yet ever rid of his burden by him; no, nor ever is like to be: ye cannot be justified by the works of the law; for by the deeds of the law no man living can be rid of his burden: Therefore Mr. Worldly Wiseman is an alien, and Mr. Legality is a cheat; and for his son Civility, notwithstanding his simpering looks, he is but a hypocrite, and cannot help you. Believe me, there is nothing in all this noise that you hast heard of these sottish men, but a design to beguile you of your salvation, by turning you from the way in which I had set you. After this, Evangelist called aloud to the heavens for confirmation of what he had said; and with that there came words and fire out of the mountain under which poor Christian stood, which made the hair of his flesh stand up. The words were pronounced: "As many as are of the works of the law,

are under the curse; for it is written, Cursed is every one that continues not in all things which are written in the book of the law to do them." Gal. 3:10.

Now Christian looked for nothing but death, and began to cry out lamentably; even cursing the time in which he met with Mr. Worldly Wiseman; still calling himself a thousand fools for hearkening to his counsel. He also was greatly ashamed to think that this gentleman's arguments, flowing only from the flesh, should have the prevalency with him so far as to cause him to forsake the right way. This done, he applied himself again to Evangelist in words and sense as follows.

Christian: Sir, what think you? Is there any hope? May I now go back, and go up to the wicket-gate? Shall I not be abandoned for this, and sent back from thence ashamed? I am sorry I have hearkened to this man's counsel; but may my sin be forgiven?

Evangelist: Then said Evangelist to him, Your sin is very great, for by it you hast committed two evils: you hast forsaken the way that is good, to tread in forbidden paths. Yet will the man at the gate receive you, for he has good-will for men; only, said he, take heed that you turn not aside again, lest you "perish from the way, when his wrath is kindled but a little." Psalm 2:12.[26]

There is a way that seems right to a man, but the end of that way is death (see Proverbs 14:12). Our job in our witness to the unsaved is to tell them that they are not to even *touch* the mountain. It will kill them. As many as are of the Law are under the curse (see Galatians 3:10). Paul said that the Commandment brought death to him (see Romans 7:7–10). It is a delusional criminal indeed who commits cruel murders and thinks that he will get help and comfort by snuggling up to the law. Rather, he will receive only wrath. It is in seeing wrath flow from the Law that we flee to mercy. It instructs us to run to the cross.

We need the moral Law to prepare the way for the gospel. Without it sinners cling to their works, thinking they will be justified by them. This can be likened to the Dunning-Kruger effect:

> The Dunning-Kruger effect is a cognitive bias in which people assess their cognitive ability as greater than it is. It is related to the cognitive bias of illusory superiority and comes from the inability of people to recognize their lack of ability. Without the self-awareness of metacognition, people cannot objectively evaluate their competence or incompetence.[27]

That is a way of saying that people who are dumb often think they are smart. Those who lack ability often believe they have ability. They watch the athlete and think they can run faster, jump higher, or leap longer. Their view of themselves is soaked in delusional human pride. This is never more true than in our estimation of our moral standing. We think we are good when we're not. And that's where this frightening but wonderful Law makes its thundering entrance. It has the ability to put the fear of God into deluded sinners and awaken them to their true state before a holy God. It is in hearing that we should have no other gods before Him that we realize we're guilty of the sin of idolatry—a violation of the First and Second Commandments. We willingly embrace an image of God as an idol of wood or stone, or as an idol of the mind. We love our little image and we cling to it because it doesn't threaten us with wrath for our sin.

I received this delightful email from a woman who was seeing the futility of trusting in a religious system rather than in the Savior:

> I came across your YouTube videos and have been watching them intently over the last number of months. I find myself at a spiritual crossroads and would be very grateful for your guidance. I am an Irish 51-year-old happily married lady with four children. I come from a Catholic family with very strong faith. I have raised my four children in the Catholic faith and my faith did not waiver even as each week over the last number of years has brought horrific scandal after scandal. I started my own investigations into the Catholic church and my findings have left me in disbelief and spiritually lost. My faith in Jesus has never faltered but how I practice my faith, i.e., mass, reciting prayers, etc., has left me so confused and lost. I went so far as to go to a local Christian church recently but that didn't feel right either.
>
> I would be grateful for any advice or direction you could offer me. I love your message and your preaching but I just no longer know how to live my faith.

My advice to her was the same as the advice of Evangelist to Christian in *Pilgrim's Progress*—to follow the light. Instead of listing the failings in her religion, I told her to simply study the New Testament. God was already opening her eyes to the truth, so I said I would pray that He would direct her, knowing that in His faithfulness He would.

TAKING GOD'S NAME IN VAIN

The Third Commandment is, "You shall not take the name of the LORD your God in vain, for the LORD will not hold him guiltless who takes His name in vain" (Exodus 20:7).

151

In reference to the Third Commandment, some contend that the meaning of "in vain" doesn't mean to use it in place of a cuss word.

Dennis Pragar said,

The worst sin is committing evil in God's name. How do we know?

From the third of the Ten Commandments. This is the only one of the ten that states that God will not forgive a person who violates the commandment. What does this commandment say?

It is most commonly translated as, "Do not take the name of the Lord thy God in vain. For the Lord will not hold guiltless"—meaning "will not forgive"—"whoever takes His name in vain."

Because of this translation, most people understandably think that the commandment forbids saying God's name for no good reason. So, something like, "God, did I have a rough day at work today!" violates the third commandment.

But that interpretation presents a real problem. It would mean that whereas God could forgive the violation of any of the other commandments—dishonoring one's parents, stealing, adultery or even committing murder—He would never forgive someone who said, "God, did I have a rough day at work today!"

Let's be honest: That would render God and the Ten Commandments morally incomprehensible.

As it happens, however, the commandment is not the problem. The problem is the translation. The Hebrew original doesn't say "Do not take"; it says "Do not carry." The Hebrew literally reads, "Do not carry the name of the Lord thy God in vain."

This is reflected in one of the most widely used new translations of the Bible, the New International Version, or NIV, which uses the word "misuse" rather than the word "take:" "You shall not misuse the name of the Lord your God." This is much closer to the original's intent.

What does it mean to "carry" or to "misuse" God's name? It means committing evil in God's name. And that God will not forgive.[28]

TAKING GOD'S NAME IN VAIN MEANS TO COUNT IT AS NOTHING. IT IS A FAILURE TO GIVE IT DUE RESPECT.

According to Jesus, Mr. Pragar is mistaken. *Every* sin but blasphemy against the Holy Spirit is forgivable:

"Assuredly, I say to you, all sins will be forgiven the sons of men, and whatever blasphemies they may utter; but he who blasphemes against the Holy Spirit never has forgiveness, but is subject to eternal condemnation." (Mark 3:28,29)

Taking God's name in vain means to count it as nothing. It is a failure to give it due respect. It means to let it roll off your sinful tongue as though it were worthless, as the website GotQuestions.org confirms:

Although many people believe taking the Lord's name in vain refers to using the Lord's name as a swear word, there is much more involved with a vain use of God's name. To understand the severity of taking the Lord's name in vain, we must first see the Lord's name from His perspective as outlined in Scripture. The God of Israel was known by many names and titles, but the concept embodied in God's name plays an important and unique role in the Bible. God's nature and attributes, the totality of His being, and especially His glory are reflected in His name (Psalm 8:1). Psalm 111:9 tells us His name is "holy and awesome," and the Lord's prayer begins by addressing God with the phrase "hallowed be your name" (Matthew 6:9), an indication that a reverence for God and His name should be foremost in our prayers…

Because of the greatness of the name of God, any use of God's name that brings dishonor on Him or on His character is taking His name in vain. The third of the Ten Commandments forbids taking or using the Lord's name in an irreverent manner because that would indicate a lack of respect for God Himself.[29]

The Fourth Commandment says,

Remember the Sabbath day, to keep it holy. Six days you shall labor and do all your work, but the seventh day is the Sabbath of the LORD your God. In it you shall do no work: you, nor your son, nor your daughter, nor your male servant, nor your female servant, nor your cattle, nor your stranger who is within your gates. For in six days the LORD made the heavens and the earth, the sea, and all that is in them, and rested the seventh day. Therefore the LORD blessed the Sabbath day and hallowed it. (Exodus 20:8–11)

We cannot separate the other commandments from the First. To have no other Gods before Him means that we love Him above all else, and that means we honor Him by setting aside a special day to rest, because He tells us to do that. It is a day in which we cease to labor.

There are some who say that Christians are therefore to keep the Jewish Sabbath, which means that we should *gather for fellowship* on that day. But the Fourth Commandment doesn't tell us to gather in worship; it instructs us to rest.

Scripture tells us that early Christians kept the first day of the week:

> Now on the first day of the week, when the disciples came together to break bread, Paul, ready to depart the next day, spoke to them and continued his message until midnight. (Acts 20:7)

> On the first day of the week let each one of you lay something aside, storing up as he may prosper, that there be no collections when I come. (1 Corinthians 16:2)

ARE WE OBLIGATED?

The question often arises from Seventh Day Adventists as to why Christians don't keep the Jewish Sabbath. They argue that Jesus kept the Sabbath and we should also, because He is our example. Here is a typical comment:

> Read Mark 1:21, Mark 6:2, Luke 4:16–30, Luke 6:6–11, Luke 13:10–16,Luke 14:1–5. What do these texts teach us about Jesus and the Sabbath? As you read them, ask yourself where, if anywhere, you can find indications that Jesus was either abolishing our obligation to keep the Sabbath or pointing to another day to replace it?
>
> Why should we make it our custom to go to church on Sabbath, as Jesus went to the synagogue on Sabbath?
>
> *"As His custom was"* (Luke 4:16, NKJV). Only Luke uses this phrase: in Luke 4:16, as Jesus attended the synagogue in Nazareth; and in Luke 22:39, as the cross drew

near, Jesus went, *as was his custom, to the Mount of Olives* (RSV). Both times the *"custom"* had to do with worship and prayer.[30]

They also point to the disciples and to the apostle Paul, who went to the synagogue on the Sabbath:

PAUL ENTERED THE SYNAGOGUES ON THE SABBATH TO *REASON* WITH THE JEWS ABOUT JESUS, NOT TO KEEP THE SABBATH.

There are many scriptures that verify the Sabbath day being the 7th day of the week. All throughout the 'New testament,' the first day of the week is called "The first day of the week" and the 7th day of the week is called "The Sabbath." This fact alone should prove when the Sabbath truly is.

However, let us examine the pattern of the disciples after Yahushua's resurrection in the book of acts to determine what day that they attended Sabbath Services and what day they expected others to observe. We will keep a count of how many times the Sabbath is observed.

We see one example in Acts 17:1 ...

Acts 17:1 (NKJV) Now when they had passed through Amphipolis and Apollonia, they came to Thessalonica, where there was a synagogue of the Jews. Acts 17:2 Then Paul, as his custom was, went in to them, and for three Sabbaths reasoned with them from the Scriptures, Acts 17:3 explaining and demonstrating that the Messiah had to suffer and rise again from the dead, and [saying], "This Yahushua whom I preach to you is the Messiah." Acts

> 17:4 And some of them were persuaded; and a great
> multitude of the devout Greeks, and not a few of
> the leading women, joined Paul and Silas.[31]

Some Christians use "Yahushua" (or "Yeshua") when they speak of Jesus. They use English to refer to Abraham, Moses, Joseph, or Paul, but for some reason think it's spiritual to use the Hebrew language when they refer to Jesus. However, I always use the English language when speaking of Jesus, because unbelievers (those we're trying to reach) will have no idea Who we're talking about if we refer to Him in a foreign language they don't speak. I may as well be saying, "Put your faith in Ἰησοῦς Χριστός."

Paul entered the synagogues on the Sabbath to *reason* with the Jews about Jesus, not to keep the Sabbath. In the book of Galatians he makes it abundantly clear that we cannot be saved by keeping the Law. He loved the Jews and became all things to reach them:

> For though I am free from all men, I have made myself
> a servant to all, that I might win the more; and to the
> Jews I became as a Jew, that I might win Jews; to those
> who are under the law, as under the law, that I might
> win those who are under the law; to those who are with-
> out law, as without law (not being without law toward
> God, but under law toward Christ), that I might win
> those who are without law; to the weak I became as
> weak, that I might win the weak. I have become all
> things to all men, that I might by all means save some.
> Now this I do for the gospel's sake, that I may be par-
> taker of it with you. (1 Corinthians 9:19–23)

If the Seventh Day Adventists want to follow Paul's ex-ample, they should enter synagogues each Sabbath and reason with Jews about Jesus. Instead, they go to their own church building, keep the Sabbath, and tell others we should follow *their* example. Paul didn't do that. He went to synagogues to evangelize.

Nowhere in the New Testament is there even one verse telling Christians to keep the Sabbath. If there was, I would gladly keep it. Instead, there many admonitions not to let anyone tell you what day you are to keep, and to keep the liberty we have in Christ. If Seventh Day Adventists want to have their gathering on the Sabbath, that's their liberty. However, they have no right to lay that burden on others. Romans 14 makes that clear:

> Who are you to judge another's servant? To his own master he stands or falls. Indeed, he will be made to stand, for God is able to make him stand.
>
> One person esteems one day above another; another esteems every day alike. Let each be fully convinced in his own mind. He who observes the day, observes it to the Lord; and he who does not observe the day, to the Lord he does not observe it. He who eats, eats to the Lord, for he gives God thanks; and he who does not eat, to the Lord he does not eat, and gives God thanks. For none of us lives to himself, and no one dies to himself. For if we live, we live to the Lord; and if we die, we die to the Lord.
>
> Therefore, whether we live or die, we are the Lord's. For to this end Christ died and rose and lived again, that He might be Lord of both the dead and the living. But why do you judge your brother? Or why do you show contempt for your brother? For we shall all stand before the judgment seat of Christ. (Romans 14:4–10)

Instead of keeping their Sabbath convictions to themselves, they try to lay a weight on other people's shoulders that no one can carry. When certain men told the disciples that they had to keep the Law, the apostles and elders met to discuss this subject, and here is their conclusion:

> Since we have heard that some who went out from us have troubled you with words, unsettling your souls, saying, "You must be circumcised and keep the law"— to whom we gave no such commandment—it seemed good to us, being assembled with one accord, to send chosen men to you with our beloved Barnabas and Paul, men who have risked their lives for the name of our Lord Jesus Christ. We have therefore sent Judas and Silas, who will also report the same things by word of mouth. For it seemed good to the Holy Spirit, and to us, to lay upon you no greater burden than these necessary things: that you abstain from things offered to idols, from blood, from things strangled, and from sexual immorality. If you keep yourselves from these, you will do well. (Acts 15:24–29)

So stand fast in the liberty you have in Christ, and don't let anyone unsettle you, because that's what Sabbath keepers try to do.

The Fifth Commandment says,

> Honor your father and your mother, that your days may be long upon the land which the LORD your God is giving you. (Exodus 20:12)

Have we always honored our parents implicitly, treating them in a way that's pleasing to God? This doesn't mean we honor them only if we think they are good parents. We are to honor them because they are our parents. If you're not born again, ask God to remind you of the sins of your youth. You may have forgotten them, but God hasn't.

WHEN MURDER IS ACCEPTABLE

The Sixth Commandment is, "You shall not murder" (Exodus 20:13).

The Bible warns that if we are angry at someone without cause we are in danger of judgment (Matthew 5:22), and that "whoever hates his brother is a murderer" (1 John 3:15). We can violate God's Law simply by our attitude and intent. Many times I have heard people say, when challenged about their sin, "Well, I've never murdered anyone," not realizing that in God's eyes they have. Social media is filled with vile, hate-filled comments, as well as actual death threats, each of which constitutes murder according to God's holy standard.

In addition, we often hear of people killing for the most petty of reasons. For example, some have flown into a murderous rage simply by being "unfriended" on Facebook, being forced to play a boring board game, or being served a poorly cooked pork chop![32] There's such an appalling lack of respect for life in our nation. When you think contemporary humanity has scraped the bottom of the barrel, it goes even deeper into depravity. Late in 2019, a man in Great Britain tossed his mother off a balcony, killing her, because she had Alzheimer's. The judge gave him a suspended sentence and praised his act of "love."

I interviewed numerous college students to get their thoughts on the incident, and many either agreed with the son's actions or were unable to say what he did was wrong. Yet when asked about Sam Little, America's most prolific serial killer who strangled ninety-three women and said he enjoyed every one, those same individuals couldn't justify the death penalty for a mass murderer! (See the details in our shocking video, "When It's Okay to Kill Your Mother.")

America is also guilty of a terrible sin that is often swept to the side. When we think of the Sixth Commandment and cite statistics of how many murders take place in our country each year, we forget that abortion is the killing of babies in the womb. Since *Roe v. Wade* legalized abortion in 1973, approximately 60 million precious unborn children have been murdered.

Each one is a living human being, created in the image of God, with a beating heart at twenty-one days and measurable brainwaves at forty days, yet its body is crushed or torn limb from limb and then ripped from the womb.

A woman scientist who advocated for abortion rights changed her mind after seeing the destructive influence in the lives of those who had had an abortion:

In an astonishingly candid Twitter thread, Rachel Bock wrote that she "grew up progressive, pro-choice all the way" and never really considered any other viewpoint when it came to the controversial subject and had been told that the pro-choice position "was the only moral conclusion."

However, Bock then went through a series of personal experiences that made her question the very tenets of her view on the termination of pregnancy and the destruction of human life.

The first situation that shifted Rachel's perspective involved her own brother.

"My brother got a girl pregnant when he was 19. We all wanted her to abort, please!" Bock wrote. "This was clearly horrible. She didn't. My niece, now 17, is a shining light in this world. Her smile & presence lights up everyone around her. It's amazing. The hindsight on this is palpable."

Then, a close friend of hers decided to get an abortion after falling pregnant at just 17.

"I drove her and waited for her," Bock wrote. "She still lights a candle for the child on the would-be birthday. I think this has contributed to her struggle with depression, which she has gone in and out of since then."...

Summing up her change of heart, the scientist wrote that she has "not known a woman in my life without some degree of psychological issue after aborting" and had "never met someone who kept the child and then regretted it. Even when they thought they really really didn't want a kid."[33]

SUCH TEPID MORALITY IS THE RESULT OF THE REMOVAL OF GOD'S LAW FROM THE EQUATION.

We have been so conditioned by the thought that abortion is acceptable that we can think what this woman is saying is wonderful when it's not. Imagine if I said, "I was once an advocate for the killing of a spouse. I thought it was the right of every husband to murder his wife for any reason. But I was wrong. I've come to see that when a man kills his wife it leaves him feeling guilty. He has emotional fallout after he kills her."

Is murder wrong simply because it leaves the murderer unhappy? Of course not. Murder is wrong because it's evil. It is a violation of the Sixth Commandment, and those who spill the precious blood of another human being through murder sin again God and will incur His wrath. Such tepid morality is the result of the removal of God's Law from the equation.

INHERITING THE KINGDOM

The Seventh Commandment is, "You shall not commit adultery" (Exodus 20:14).

As with the Sixth Commandment, we don't have to commit the physical act to be guilty before God. Who of us can say that we are pure of heart? Jesus warned, "Whoever looks at a woman to lust for her has already committed adultery with her in his heart" (Matthew 5:28). God sees every thought we have and every sin we have ever committed. The day will come when we will have to face His Law, and we are told that the impure, fornicators (those who have sex before marriage), and adulterers will not enter the Kingdom of God (1 Corinthians 6:9,10). Proverbs 6:23 says, "Whoever commits adultery with a woman lacks understanding; he who does so destroys his own soul."

The Eighth Commandment is, "You shall not steal" (Exodus 20:15). Most people think of stealing as taking an item from a store and believe they're off the hook if they haven't done that. Or they'll say that they only stole once, when they were a child. But time doesn't forgive sin. God sees the sins of yesterday as if they were committed today.

Consider whether you have ever taken anything that didn't belong to you, regardless of its value. This includes pocketing a pack of gum at a store, as well as stealing an answer on a test, taking a pen from work, even keeping extra change that you know isn't rightfully yours. If you've taken anything that doesn't belong to you, then you are a thief—and you cannot enter God's Kingdom (1 Corinthians 6:10).

The Ninth Commandment is, "You shall not bear false witness against your neighbor" (Exodus 20:16).

People often try to justify their dishonesty by saying they have told only "white lies." But there is no difference between a white lie, a half-truth, a fib, or an exaggeration. All are lies in the sight of God. Just as someone has to commit only one murder to be a murderer, telling only one lie, no matter what color or size, makes us a liar.

Numbers 23:19 tells us, "God is not a man, that He should lie." Because He is a God of truth and holiness, His Law demands absolute honesty. We may not think deceitfulness is a serious sin, but God does. "Lying lips are an abomination to the Lord" (Proverbs 12:22), and the Bible warns that all liars will have their part in the Lake of Fire (Revelation 21:8).

Last, the Tenth Commandment says,

> You shall not covet your neighbor's house; you shall not covet your neighbor's wife, nor his male servant, nor his female servant, nor his ox, nor his donkey, nor anything that is your neighbor's. (Exodus 20:17)

Coveting seems like such a minor sin. But consider that before Achan stole some of the spoils of Jericho, he "coveted them and took them" (Joshua 7:20,21), bringing destruction upon him and his family. Before David committed adultery with Bathsheba, then had her husband killed, he coveted his neighbor's wife. Covetousness opens the door to jealousy, greed, lust, and a host of other sins. That's why Jesus warned, "Take heed and beware of covetousness..." (Luke 12:15).

Have you ever coveted (jealously desired) anything that belongs to another person? That's a violation of the Tenth Commandment, and the covetous will not inherit the Kingdom of God (Ephesians 5:5).

CHAPTER Ten

NEVER LOSE
SIGHT OF MOSES

After hearing all the words that God spoke, the Israelites were rightly fearful at what they saw and heard.

> Now all the people witnessed the thunderings, the lightning flashes, the sound of the trumpet, and the mountain smoking; and when the people saw it, they trembled and stood afar off. Then they said to Moses, "You speak with us, and we will hear; but let not God speak with us, lest we die." (Exodus 20:18,19)

If you are unsaved, "hear" Moses. Listen to the Law. Let it expose and condemn you. Allow it to give you light before it flushes you out and judges you guilty. If you are saved, give Moses to sinners. Let them hear the thunder and see the lightning flashes.

Someone emailed me these encouraging words:

> I used the method that you used, Mr. Comfort, and I cannot help but praise God for what He did on my co-worker!!!! I had asked him if he thinks he is a good person. He said yes. I just asked him one question, if he has ever lied, he IMMEDIATELY thought for a minute, and to my surprise, and joy, he said, "I am a terrible per-

son!" I was literally rejoicing and praising God!! I continued witnessing, and showed him how the Bible teaches of Christ, and what He did on the cross. What surprised me even more was when I finished talking to him, he did the "mind-blowing" hand motion and said that what I had told him was "mind blowing"! Pray for my coworker please that God would save his soul!!!

The Ten Commandments that are written by God's finger on tablets of stone are the same Law that is written on the hearts of all mankind. Let it speak to the sinner and do its convicting work on the conscience.

IT IS THE FEAR OF THE LORD THAT PERPETUALLY CAUSES US TO DEPART FROM EVIL (PROVERBS 16:6).

And Moses said to the people, "Do not fear; for God has come to test you, and that His fear may be before you, so that you may not sin." (Exodus 20:20)

At face value, these are strange words: "Do not fear...that His fear may be before you."

Jesus said similar things. He said, "Fear not," and then said to fear Him who can cast body and soul into Hell. One fear is a trembling that results from a lack of trust, and the other fear is the beginning of wisdom. It is the second fear that we should embrace. It is the fear of the Lord that perpetually causes us to depart from evil (Proverbs 16:6). It continually keeps us from giving ourselves to lust and every other sin that our evil heart desires.

So the people stood afar off, but Moses drew near the thick darkness where God was.

Then the LORD said to Moses, "Thus you shall say to the children of Israel: 'You have seen that I have talked with you from heaven. You shall not make anything to be with Me—gods of silver or gods of gold you shall not make for yourselves. An altar of earth you shall make for Me, and you shall sacrifice on it your burnt offerings and your peace offerings, your sheep and your oxen. In every place where I record My name I will come to you, and I will bless you. And if you make Me an altar of stone, you shall not build it of hewn stone; for if you use your tool on it, you have profaned it. Nor shall you go up by steps to My altar, that your nakedness may not be exposed on it.'" (Exodus 20:21–26)

THE ROOT OF ALL SIN

After many years of pleading with sinners to come to the cross, I have come to the conclusion that idolatry is at the root of all sin. This is based on the fact that God saw fit to address this sin in the first two of the Ten Commandments. Men love darkness and stay in darkness, because they don't fear God. And they don't fear God because they don't see Him as He is. To them, He is not surrounded by thunder, lightning, and thick smoke. The thought of His voice doesn't make them tremble in terror. It doesn't cause them to listen to Moses, and Jesus said that if they don't listen to Moses, neither will they listen if one rises from the dead (Luke 16:31). And because they don't understand His holiness, they think that they can climb the Hill of Morality to make it to Heaven. Or they try to justify themselves by pointing to the moral flaws in their idol.

Then there are those who seem intent on going to Hell and seem to strive diligently to make sure that they get there.

This includes making up "What if" scenarios—one of which is the ever-popular, "*What if* Hitler gave his heart to Jesus just before he died?" Then they come to their own conclusions about the moral character of God in supposedly saving him, while sending other people to Hell who haven't killed a flea, let alone a soul. It is too harsh. It is, therefore, the "evil" character of God that they believe justly stops them from coming to Christ. In reality, it's their love of sin that stops them.

What happened to Hitler is of no concern to us. That's God's business, not ours. What we do know is that "the judgments of the LORD are true and righteous altogether" (Psalm 19:9). He is without sin. Absolute righteousness will be done on Judgment Day. So I need not be concerned that God is slightly unjust, let alone that He's evil.

Any surmising about who He has saved and why will produce endless speculation. He saves all who come to Him in repentance and faith, and He alone knows who is genuinely repentant and who is not. We should spend our time praying for and pleading with the unsaved rather than asking questions like how many pins can fit on the head of an angel. Look at how Scripture encourages us to use our precious time wisely:

> As I urged you when I was on my way to Macedonia, stay on at Ephesus so that you may instruct certain individuals not to teach any different doctrines, nor to pay attention to legends (fables, myths) and endless genealogies, which give rise to useless speculation and meaningless arguments rather than advancing God's program of instruction which is grounded in faith [and requires surrendering the entire self to God in absolute trust and confidence]. (1 Timothy 1:3,4, AMP)

There is the answer to how we should handle the endless "What ifs." We have confidence in God's integrity. We trust Him. That's an easy baby-step for the humble, but it's a great leap that the proud of heart refuse to take, because they don't want to go there. They want rather to stay in their beloved and pleasurable sins, and the end of that will be damnation under the wrath of a holy, just, and perfect Law.

More fodder for the proud of heart is the Second Commandment, which we looked at earlier:

> ...you shall not bow down to them nor serve them. For I, the LORD your God, am a jealous God, visiting the iniquity of the fathers upon the children to the third and fourth generations of those who hate Me, but showing mercy to thousands, to those who love Me and keep My commandments. (Exodus 20:5,6)

Here is "evidence" that there is more than one God, and that He is sinful in that He gets jealous, which proves He is petty. Plus, He is unjust in what they see as punishing precious children for the sins of their fathers.

However, this is not an unjust punishment of innocent children for their father's sins, but just punishment upon those who hate God. He gave them life, and they hate Him without cause. Godless fathers reproduce their own kind, and their own kind reap wrath for their own sin—unless they come to the Savior and receive His mercy.

GONE FOR TOO LONG

While Moses is up on the mountain, something strange happens with the people below:

> Now when the people saw that Moses delayed coming down from the mountain, the people gathered together

to Aaron, and said to him, "Come, make us gods that shall go before us; for as for this Moses, the man who brought us up out of the land of Egypt, we do not know what has become of him."

And Aaron said to them, "Break off the golden earrings which are in the ears of your wives, your sons, and your daughters, and bring them to me." So all the people broke off the golden earrings which were in their ears, and brought them to Aaron. And he received the gold from their hand, and he fashioned it with an engraving tool, and made a molded calf.

Then they said, "This is your god, O Israel, that brought you out of the land of Egypt!"

So when Aaron saw it, he built an altar before it. And Aaron made a proclamation and said, "Tomorrow is a feast to the LORD." Then they rose early on the next day, offered burnt offerings, and brought peace offerings; and the people sat down to eat and drink, and rose up to play. (Exodus 32:1–6)

This would seem to be a mystery, because God Himself had just given the children of Israel the Ten Commandments, the first two of which forbade making graven images. It's also hard to understand how Aaron could have been complicit in such blatant sin. But there are important and powerful truths in this incident.

Whenever we (as a church or as a nation) forget Moses, we lose sight of the Law. In doing so, we naturally create an idol—and even leaders are unwittingly involved. This is because a golden calf is attractive. We "rise early" to be involved, because an idol has no conditional morality. It gives permission to rise up and play. It offers a form of godliness but it allows us to hold on to our beloved sins. Plus, it appeases the guilty conscience because it accepts religious works. We willingly give our golden earrings. We don't tremble at sin or trust alone in grace. Such is the delusion of those who create their own image of God.

Again, when we lose sight of Moses, sin is no longer defined. Without the Law there is no knowledge of sin (see Romans 3:20; 7:7). It's not seen as being exceedingly sinful (see Romans 7:13), and so we get professing Christians who maintain that repentance isn't necessary for salvation. They say that if we preach repentance (as Jesus, John the Baptist, and Paul did), we are preaching salvation by works, and that's heresy. They maintain that all a sinner needs to do is *believe*, and they have out-of-context verses to back up their claims that *faith* alone is necessary. And yet in the context of salvation, we are saved by grace alone *through* faith. We are not saved *because* we believe. Believing (having faith) is merely the avenue by which grace saves us:

WHENEVER WE (AS A CHURCH OR AS A NATION) FORGET MOSES, WE LOSE SIGHT OF THE LAW.

> For by grace you have been saved *through faith*, and that not of yourselves; it is the gift of God, not of works, lest anyone should boast. (Ephesians 2:8,9)

The famous hymn is called "Amazing *Grace*," not "Amazing Faith." We are the ones who have faith. But it's God who offers grace that saves wretches like you and me.

Look at how Charles Spurgeon tells sinners to turn from sin:

> If thou be a real seeker, the hands that have been stained with lust shall one day grasp the harp of gold, and the

head that has plotted against the Most High shall yet be girt with gold. Seems it not a strange thing that God should do so much for sinners? But strange though it seem, it shall be strangely true. Look at the staggering drunkard in the ale-house. Is there a possibility that one day he shall stand among the fairest sons of light? Possibility! ay, certainty, if he repents and turns from the error of his ways. Hear you yon curser and swearer? See you the man who labels himself as a servant of hell, and is not ashamed to do so? Is it possible that he shall one day share the bliss of the redeemed? Possible! ay, more, it is sure, if he turns from his evil ways. O sovereign grace, turn men that they may repent! "Turn ye, turn ye, why will ye die, O house of Israel?"[34]

In July 2019, a woman called my name as I was parking my bike in the garage. She was standing meekly in our driveway, so I approached her to find that she was deeply concerned about her twenty-something son, who was seriously depressed. She considered me to be "a man of God" and asked if I would talk with him.

About ten minutes later I was in her home, talking to her son. David listened as I shared the gospel, politely took one of my books and other literature, and then told me he was busy. That was a little awkward because I knew that he wasn't. He was "busy" sitting in his bedroom most of the day. I asked, "Are you kicking me out?" He said that he wasn't, but that he had things to do. So I left, much to the disappointment of his mother.

Two weeks later our doorbell rang. Twice. It was the young man. He was humble, apologetic about how he had treated me, and contrite about his sins. He wanted to get right with God, and asked, "Will God accept me? I have said some horrible things to Him." I told him that God was rich in mercy, able to "save to the uttermost," assuring him that he wasn't alone—that millions say horrible things to and about Him every day with their blasphemy. The two truths I emphasized were repentance and faith, in that order:

> "The time is fulfilled, and the kingdom of God is at hand. *Repent, and believe in the gospel.*" (Mark 1:15)

If a sinner merely believes but doesn't repent—that is, he continues to lie, steal, lust, fornicate, etc.—all he is doing is playing the hypocrite and deceiving himself. Scripture is very clear about the necessity of departing from sin when professing faith in Jesus:

> Let everyone who names the name of Christ *depart from iniquity*. (2 Timothy 2:19)

I then gave David some literature (including our booklet "Save Yourself Some Pain," which contains principles of Christian growth), prayed with him, and told him that God would be as real to him as he would be with God.

CHAPTER *Eleven*

MOSES AND JESUS

Moses was a sinner. Unlike Joseph and a few others in Scripture, his sin is made bare at times—from his anger, to his fears, to his unbelief at the burning bush—and yet he was privileged like no other person in Scripture. He spoke with God "face to face, as a man speaks to his friend" (Exodus 33:11). However, his life is more than a series of blessed events, as we have seen. It was a foreshadowing of Jesus. In Deuteronomy 18:15 Moses said,

> "The LORD your God will raise up for you a Prophet like me from your midst, from your brethren. Him you shall hear..."

Both Moses and Jesus were born under foreign domination. Both had rulers try to kill them just after they were born (see Exodus 1:15–22; Matthew 2:16–18). Both of them were shepherds, fasted for forty days, and were said to be humble (see Numbers 12:3; Matthew 11:29).

The tabernacle was the dwelling place of Almighty God, but consider how the children of Israel looked to Moses as he entered the tabernacle:

So it was, whenever Moses went out to the tabernacle, that all the people rose, and each man stood at his tent door and watched Moses until he had gone into the tabernacle. And it came to pass, when Moses entered the tabernacle, that the pillar of cloud descended and stood at the door of the tabernacle, and the LORD talked with Moses. All the people saw the pillar of cloud standing at the tabernacle door, and all the people rose and worshiped, each man in his tent door. So the LORD spoke to Moses face to face, as a man speaks to his friend. (Exodus 33:8–11)

We, as Christians, are told to look "unto Jesus, the author and finisher of our faith" (Hebrews 12:2). He was the One who entered into the presence of God to obtain our redemption. Here we're told God spoke to Moses "face to face." In other words, He spoke intimately, as you would with a friend.

Moses is very bold. He walked in the fear of God, and in that fear he had the liberty to express his heart, make bold statements, and ask his Creator bold questions . . . all leading up to the boldest of all. This is how that intimate conversation went:

Then Moses said to the LORD, "See, You say to me, 'Bring up this people.' But You have not let me know whom You will send with me. Yet You have said, 'I know you by name, and you have also found grace in My sight.' Now therefore, I pray, if I have found grace in Your sight, show me now Your way, that I may know You and that I may find grace in Your sight. And consider that this nation is Your people."

And He said, "My Presence will go with you, and I will give you rest."

Then he said to Him, "If Your Presence does not go with us, do not bring us up from here. For how then will it be known that Your people and I have found grace in Your sight, except You go with us? So we shall be separate, Your people and I, from all the people who are upon the face of the earth."

So the LORD said to Moses, "I will also do this thing that you have spoken; for you have found grace in My sight, and I know you by name." (Exodus 33:12–17)

Here is that boldest of requests:

And he said, "Please, show me Your glory." (v. 18)

Moses had seen different manifestations of the Creator. But now he asked to see what no man had seen nor could see. He was asking to see light that was above the brightness of the sun. That light shined a little on Saul of Tarsus on the Damascus road, and blinded him for life but for the healing grace of God that gave him back his sight. But Moses wanted to see His glory, and in God's answer we see why no human being could be in the immediate presence of Almighty God:

Then He said, "I will make all My goodness pass before you, and I will proclaim the name of the LORD before you. I will be gracious to whom I will be gracious, and I will have compassion on whom I will have compassion." But He said, "You cannot see My face; for no man shall see Me, and live." (Exodus 33:19,20)

Often we hear skeptics say things like, "The Bible is filled with mistakes, proving that it is not God's Word." There *are* mistakes in the Bible—but they're man's mistakes, not God's. For example, skeptics point to the fact that the Scriptures say there is not a righteous man on the face of the earth (Romans 3:10), and at the same time we find individuals like Job being called "blameless" (Job 1:1). However, people can be blameless because they offer a sacrificial lamb for a temporary covering for their sins. They are without *blame* in the sight of God for their transgressions, but they are not without sin (see Romans 3:23). Skeptics also point to verses saying no man has seen God at any time (John 1:18), and yet Jacob said that he had seen God face to face (Genesis 32:30).

However, the statement "face to face" is anthropomorphic. God is a Spirit. He doesn't have physical hands, fingers, eyes, and a face as do His creatures. When the Bible says that the eye of the Lord is in every place, it doesn't mean that God has a physical eye. It simply means that God sees everything. These are spiritual attributes and features that give us some understanding of things we could normally never grasp. Jacob hadn't seen the essence of God; he had seen a physical manifestation. We see the same thing here when God spoke to Moses "face to face" as with a friend (intimately), yet Moses could not see His face and live. Instead, God let him see only a glimpse of His glory:

> And the LORD said, "Here is a place by Me, and you shall stand on the rock. So it shall be, while My glory passes by, that I will put you in the cleft of the rock, and will cover you with My hand while I pass by. Then I will take away My hand, and you shall see My back; but My face shall not be seen." (Exodus 33:21–23)

Moses asked to see God's glory, and God called His glory His "goodness." It was more than light that would kill the offspring of Adam; it was His terrifying "goodness." It is the goodness of a judge that will send a heinous criminal to the gallows. It is his goodness that motivates him to see that justice is done. His wrath is according to his goodness. Any judge who isn't angry at a man who has raped and cut the throats of teenage girls isn't a good judge. The greater his goodness, the greater his anger.

So it is with the Judge of all the earth. He is wrath-filled at murderers, rapists, thieves, and liars. His wrath abides on them (see John 3:36). If sinful man stood in the immediate presence of the Creator, wrath would fall on him like livid lightning. And that would be humanity's fate if God wasn't merciful.

Mercy is a dam that is holding back the fury of God, and our sobering and fearful task is to tell sinful man that time is cracking it by the minute.

THE NEVER-ENDING WILDERNESS

We can be tempted to ask why it was that God didn't take the shortcut, and just guide the children of Israel straight into the promised land. It sure would have been easier for all concerned, including Moses. Why did they have to suffer hunger and thirst in the wilderness? There's no question that He loved them, that He cared for them and led them through the dryness of that barren land.

We can also be tempted to ask why it is that life has enough pains, without God leading us into even more suffering. This is a valid question.

In an effort to address the issue of suffering, let me say that I believe in the power of prayer. My wife had horrible headaches for many years. Sometimes they were so painful they brought her to tears. Yet every night we continued to seek God to take them away. We believe in the biblical principle of importunity. I know a young man named Brandon who had an aneurysm when he was age sixteen. He was paralyzed from the neck down and wasn't able to talk or eat solid food for years.

Brandon loves the Lord but lives in a continual wilderness. Although I pray for his healing every night, I also believe that God is sovereign and that His ways are past finding out (Romans 11:33). Disease, pain, suffering, and death exist because of the Genesis Fall, so I have no problem with *why* suffering exists. My problem is that God *allows* continued suffering for millions who live in daily agony. Even though it's a mystery, that doesn't shake my faith because I see that He allowed Job to suffer. He allowed the disciples to be martyred, and He did nothing to stop Stephen from being horribly murdered.

I don't understand God's ways, but I do have faith in His precious promises. He cannot lie, and I have His immutable promise that all things work together for my good (Romans 8:28). *All* things. Therefore I give Him thanks in and for suffering. But at the same time I never give up in prayer for an end to it.

IT IS THE CROSS THAT IS LIGHT IN MY DARKNESS. WITHOUT THAT LIGHT, I WOULD BE IN DESPAIR.

There is something that glues all the thoughts on suffering together. It's the cross. It is in the cross that I see His great love for me. It is undeniable evidence that He cares for me, and gives me an anchor for my soul in the most violent of storms. It is the cross that is light in my darkness. Without that light, I would be in despair.

I never forget that millions of lost sinners live in the agony of *hopeless* despair. They don't have the consolation I have. Such a thought lifts self-pity off my shoulders and compels me to reach out with the hope of the gospel. The knowledge of their hopeless suffering and of their terrifying eternal fate helps me to bring my pains in this short life into perspective and to say with Paul in his sufferings, "His grace is sufficient for me."

WHAT WOULD YOU DO?

You're walking near an intersection, and you notice that the traffic lights are stuck on green in both directions. You look to the right and see a car rapidly approaching the intersection, obviously confident that he has the green light. You look in front of you and see another car speeding toward the intersection about the same distance away, equally certain that he has the green light. You know there's going to be a fatality— someone is about to be killed if you don't do something. You have a choice:

- You could walk away and pretend you didn't see the lights.

- You could call 911 and ask them to send a coroner because somebody is going to be dead in about ten seconds.

- You could run out into the intersection, waving your arms like a raving lunatic, and try to get the cars to stop before they crash. In doing so, you would put your life on the line for complete strangers.

You really have no choice. If you are a caring human being, you *have* to run into that intersection and put your life on the line, hoping that these strangers will believe you and stop.

And there is the dilemma you and I have with the ungodly. They are going to have a collision with God's Law, and when that happens they will perish.

We have three choices:

- We can do nothing. This is something most of the church is doing.

- We can pray about it. Some in the church pray about the unsaved.

- We can run into this world and warn them, praying that they will believe us and not see us as a raving lunatic. May we do that daily.

CHAPTER *Twelve*

WHEN YOUR
SON ASKS YOU

G od loves His Law. How could He not? The moral Law
is the manifestation of His very nature. We can no more
separate holiness, righteousness, justice, and truth from God
than we can separate water from the oceans. And so Moses
reiterates to a rebellious, dull-of-hearing nation the Ten Commandments (Deuteronomy 5:6–21), beginning with:

> "The LORD talked with you face to face on the mountain
> from the midst of the fire. I stood between the LORD
> and you at that time, to declare to you the word of the
> LORD; for you were afraid because of the fire, and you
> did not go up the mountain." (Deuteronomy 5:4,5)

After reviewing the Law he went on to say:

> "Now this is the commandment, and these are the
> statutes and judgments which the LORD your God has
> commanded to teach you, that you may observe them
> in the land which you are crossing over to possess."
> (Deuteronomy 6:1)

Then he said that the purpose of observing the Law was
"that you may fear the LORD your God, to keep all His stat-

183

utes and His commandments which I command you, you and your son and your grandson, all the days of your life, and that your days may be prolonged" (vv. 2,3). He then summed up the essence of the Law:

"Hear, O Israel: The LORD our God, the LORD is one! You shall love the LORD your God with all your heart, with all your soul, and with all your strength." (vv. 4,5)

And he added, "And these words which I command you today shall be in your heart. You shall teach them diligently to your children" (v. 7). He then became more specific in how and when they should be taught. The children of Israel should "talk of them when you sit in your house, when you walk by the way, when you lie down, and when you rise up. You shall bind them as a sign on your hand, and they shall be as frontlets between your eyes. You shall write them on the doorposts of your house and on your gates" (Deuteronomy 6:8,9).

God gave His moral Law so that the whole world—not just the children of Israel, but the whole world, *including our beloved children*—would be guilty before God (see Romans 3:19,20). So do what Scripture commands. Teach the Ten Commandments to your children from the moment of understanding. Talk of them when you sit in your house, when you walk by the way, when you lie down, and when you rise up. Bind them as a sign on your hand, between your eyes, and write them on the doorposts of your house and on your gates. In other words, get the Commandments into their minds and hearts. Why? Because it will produce the precious fruit of guilt. That's its function. It should show them and us that we need the Savior. It prepares the way of the Lord, as an informative tutor, to bring us to Christ. So many misguided parents forget the Law and give their children the cross with no knowledge of sin. The children abide in a church until the hormones kick in, the opposite sex becomes more attractive than Noah's ark, and they leave the church— much to the dismay and confusion of the parents. This is predictable when they are left without the knowledge of sin.

How different would things be if these verses were taken to heart and children grew up knowing that lust is adultery and hatred is murder, that all liars and thieves will end up damned in Hell. How different things would be if the Law was used to produce a healthy fear of God, so that every decision is made in light of our Maker. A child, left in the dark as to the true nature of sin, doesn't fear when a lie passes through his sinful lips, or when lust burns in his heart and wants control of his eyes. He doesn't pluck out his eye and cast it far from him. Instead he dulls his conscience and indulges his sinful heart.

But if he has thoroughly received instruction from the Law, as sin taunts his sin-loving heart, its weight lays guilt on his soul and brings him to the foot of the cross. This was the experience of the apostle Paul who thought that the Law would give him life, when in reality it did the opposite (see Romans 7:7–12). It killed his hope of righteousness and sent him fleeing to the Savior for mercy.

Look at what Moses then said to the children of Israel:

"When your son asks you in time to come, saying, 'What is the meaning of the testimonies, the statutes, and the judgments which the LORD our God has commanded you?' then you shall say to your son: 'We were slaves of Pharaoh in Egypt, and the LORD brought us out of Egypt with a mighty hand; and the LORD showed signs and wonders before our eyes, great and severe, against Egypt, Pharaoh, and all his household. Then He brought us out from there, that He might bring us in, to give us the land of which He swore to our fathers. And the LORD commanded us to observe all these statutes, to fear the LORD our God, for our good always, that He might preserve us alive, as it is this day. Then it will be righteousness for us, if we are careful to observe all these commandments before the LORD our God, as He has commanded us.'" (Deuteronomy 6:20–25)

THOSE WHO HAVE HAD THEIR MANY SINS FORGIVEN BY THE MERCY OF GOD TESTIFY TO HIS GLORIOUS KINDNESS.

And therein lies the wonderful fruit produced by the Law. It causes those who come through the tutor's instruction to appreciate grace. Those who have had their many sins forgiven by the mercy of God testify to His glorious kindness. They preach Christ crucified. They exalt the Savior. They ignore their fears and strive to faithfully speak of sin, righteousness, and judgment—because they fear God. He alone saved them from death and Hell and His Word is their joyful command.

SCARY ENCOUNTER

Let me tell you about one of the scariest witnessing encounters I've had. I was on a plane heading from Dallas, Texas, to Orange County in Southern California. I was seated next to a gentleman and asked what he did for a living. That's my usual plan when I witness to someone, especially in a plane. He said that he was the US General Manager of all the retailers of a well-known South Korean car manufacturer. This was a bigwig.

My plan was to speak with him during the meal when he wasn't busily answering emails and making business decisions. To my sadness, he didn't order a meal because he was going to a dinner in California. That meant he continued to work on his iPad like there was no tomorrow.

After I finished my dinner, I said, "When you have a minute, I'd like to ask you a question." Five minutes later, he turned to me and asked what I wanted to talk about. I said, "Brian, do you think there's an afterlife?" He looked a little uncomfortable, and said that his father was a Presbyterian and that he did believe in Heaven. When I asked him if he'd been born again, he said that he'd heard of it, but that he hadn't. When I told him that in John chapter 3 Jesus said that we had to be born again to enter Heaven, he responded with, "I don't know if I believe that."

He was very uncomfortable, so I decided that I would give him a way out. I said, "I know you are busy, and if you would rather not talk, I'm okay with that." He said, "This sounds like a deep conversation, and I do have a lot of work to do." When I said that I would take only three minutes, I could see him reluctantly concede. He pulled down the lid of his iPad and deliberately turned toward me.

I gathered courage and said, "Do you think you're a good person?" He replied that he tried to be, and then I began taking him through the Ten Commandments. He was hesitant but honest and admitted that he had lied, stolen, used God's name in vain (I told him that I'd heard him use it earlier). When I said, "Jesus said whoever looks at a women to lust for her has already committed adultery with her in his heart. Have you ever looked with lust?" he said that he had. That's when I said, "Brian, I'm not judging you, but you've just admitted to me that you're a lying, thieving, blasphemous adulterer at heart. If God judges you on Judgment Day by the Ten Commandments, are you going to be innocent or guilty?"

He said that he'd be guilty. "Will you go to Heaven or to Hell?" Brian confidently said that he would go to Heaven, because he tried to do good. I replied, "Try that in a court of law and it won't work. If we are guilty, doing good won't get us out of court." He quickly responded that God isn't a judge. I said that He is the *ultimate* Judge.

Around this time, I was dying inside. I had faced many a Goliath, but I couldn't help feeling intimidated by his status. I shouldn't have been, but I was. But I held onto my concern for his salvation rather than my fear of his rejection. I said, "Brian, you are like a man who is going to jump 10,000 feet out of a plane and this is your plan: you are going to try to save yourself by flapping your arms, and it's not going to work. You need to trust the parachute. By thinking you're a good person you are trying to save yourself, and you need to transfer your trust from you to the Savior. The minute you do that, God will remit your sins because of what Jesus did on the cross. You will be born again, pass from death to life, and from darkness to light. You can't earn salvation. It's too precious. It's a free gift."

I had given him quite an earful, and he had gracefully listened without interruption. I then said, "Brian, I really appreciate you listening to me. I know you've been uncomfortable, but you have been very courteous and listened. It was probably harder for me than it was for you. You may not realize this but I love you and care where you spend eternity."

On hearing that, his body language changed. I could see him relax, and he said with a touch of sincerity, "I can see you've done this before." He was right, but with this one I didn't *feel* like I had ever done it before. It was hard-going. I thanked him again for listening, and added, "I will let you get back to your work."

I then quietly thanked God that Brian had listened, and prayed that He would convict him of his sin and bring him to the cross. It will not go down on my résumé as my favorite witnessing encounter, but whether or not I enjoy sharing the gospel isn't the issue. Faithfulness is. As we came in to land, I said, "Brian, thank you for that three minutes." He gave a warm, "You're welcome. Thank you for sharing." That meant a lot. But the smile of God meant so much more. Nevertheless, I had just climbed a mountain.

CLIMBING MOUNTAINS

In Matthew chapter 18 Jesus speaks of the importance of evangelism, by likening the sinner to a lost sheep:

> "Take heed that you do not despise one of these little ones, for I say to you that in heaven their angels always see the face of My Father who is in heaven. For the Son of Man has come to save that which was lost.
>
> "What do you think? If a man has a hundred sheep, and one of them goes astray, does he not leave the ninety-nine and go to the mountains to seek the one that is straying? And if he should find it, assuredly, I say to you, he rejoices more over that sheep than over the ninety-nine that did not go astray. Even so it is not the will of your Father who is in heaven that one of these little ones should perish." (Matthew 18:10–14)

WHETHER OR NOT I ENJOY SHARING THE GOSPEL ISN'T THE ISSUE. FAITHFULNESS IS.

Look at His wording: "... does he not leave the ninety-nine and go to the *mountains* to seek the one that is straying?" Why didn't He just say, "... does he not leave the ninety-nine and seek the one that is straying?" Perhaps it's because it takes effort to climb mountains. And it's not just one mountain. Evangelism is a continual struggle. I have to daily discipline my legs to take me up those mountains. This is because there is a mountain of laziness and apathy. There is a mountain of having to *go* into the world to find sinners. There is the massive mountain of the fear of man that overshadows and intimidates me.

If we climb mountains we will fight gravity. It will always be there to push us down. And this world will always be against the task of evangelism. Unbelievers will push you down and put their foot on your neck if they can. They will discourage you in any way possible and give you what they think are good reasons to keep your mouth shut. Then there is the mountain of the spiritual battle with which we wrestle daily.

But on top of all that, there is an overshadowing Everest that keeps us going: Hell. If it didn't exist, I wouldn't care for the lost, because their lostness would be no big deal.

Here are a few more encouraging encounters from those who overcame their fears and used Moses to bring people to Jesus:

> I just wanted to let you know that I have been listening to your videos for over a year on my way to work and looking for opportunities to share the gospel. Yesterday, I had a crazy encounter with a guy in Lowe's parking lot. He offered to help me load up my car and I shared the gospel with him after the "good person test." By the end of our conversation he was in tears and knew his

need for salvation in Christ. He told me that he was going to put his faith in Christ that day and that he would have confidence in knowing that he would be in heaven when he dies. Not what I was expecting from a Lowe's trip. The guy told me that it was a miracle that I spoke with him.

Thank you for your commitment in sharing the gospel and sharing how you do it on YouTube. After watching your videos a million times, it was pretty easy to mimic how you walk through the gospel with a stranger. —Paul P.

I have a 9-year-old son named Leo. He is a precious, born-again little boy. He loves to watch videos of Ray as he witnesses to people about Jesus. About a year ago he started talking to kids on his school bus about God, the Bible, and Jesus. We call him the "bus pastor." This week he came home after school so excited. A 5th grade boy that he had been witnessing to for a few months decided to accept Jesus as his Savior. Leo led him in prayer and then brought him a New Testament the next day and has started to disciple him. This got the attention of some other boys on the bus and was met with mixed reviews. Some were interested and one of Leo's friends actually got very angry hearing about Jesus and told Leo that he is stupid to believe there is a God that created everything. Leo told him "Ray Comfort style" ... *but you believe that nothing created everything.* After that another boy asked for a New Testament because it got him thinking!

We are so amazed and blessed by how Leo is sharing the Good News of Jesus Christ with kids in a loving way that is unashamed! Glory to God and thankfulness to your awesome ministry that has touched my family's heart and better prepared us to be fishers of men!!! —Love and sincerity, Amy

This person heard the Law through our Living Waters YouTube channel:

This film [on YouTube] made me think about the reason I accepted Christ in my life. I accepted Jesus because I wanted to be accepted, I wanted to be loved. But I just prayed to God and accepted his forgiveness simply because I am tired of sinning and still justify that sin. I am tired of having hate in my heart. I am tired of lying. I am tired of being unfaithful. I am tired of being false. I want peace in my heart. This movie put a mirror in front of my face and showed me that nothing I do or say can justify anything in this world. I want to be a loving child of God. When I saw the pink-haired girl say she was suicidal it hit me hard. I prayed for her. I know I am only one person but my faith is growing stronger and if I can affect one other person in a loving way like I have seen displayed by the narrator of this video, I will be grateful to be part of God's loving plan for us all. May God bless you all and may you all truly accept God's gift of forgiveness. Amen.

We are living in dark times, so let your light shine. Talk to the lost. Genuinely love them, and let them feel your love in your tone. And if our love is genuine it will not compromise the truth, because our goal is to see sinners genuinely saved.

Look at this terribly sad news about an actor ridden with guilt for his sin, but failing to see that his sin was against

God. In May 2019, Isaac Kappy tragically took his own life at the age of forty-two. *People* magazine reported his words in his final Instagram post:

> Within the post, Kappy wrote, "Over the course of the last week, through introspection that should have happened MANY years ago, I have come to some stark revelations about my character. It is a testament to my utter arrogance that these revelations had not come sooner."
>
> "You see, I believed myself to be a good guy," he continued. "I HAVE NOT been a good guy. In fact, I have been a pretty bad guy throughout my life. I have sold drugs. I have tax delinquencies. I have debts. I have abused my body with cigarettes, drugs and alcohol. I have been abusive to people WHO LOVED ME, including my FAMILY."
>
> Kappy added he "committed an act so flippantly, without thought, that will become synonymous with short-sightedness and petty, vile greed" although he did not provide further details.
>
> The actor apologized to his friends as well, one of whom was Paris Jackson, who accused Kappy of choking her at a party they were both at in 2018.
>
> "To the MANY people I have acted abusively towards, I am very, very sorry," Kappy wrote. "To my former friends I have used and betrayed, I am sorry. To those I have deceived, I am sorry, although I must say, in my SHEER ARROGANCE, I did not even realize that I had been a bad actor all along."
>
> He continued, "I have been lacking in gratitude, humility, honor, service, and proper care for others. I have not honored the light of God within. This lesson has come too late for me, but perhaps it can inspire you."

"I will be using the remainder of my time on earth to atone for my transgressions, and to seek the light within, in others and myself," he concluded.[35]

Did that news item break your heart? Are you stirred to reach out to those who are still living, but are dying without the Savior? Are you prepared to do everything you can to reach them?

In Jesus we were given a gift we could not afford...that we cannot afford to keep. Please, give yourself away, so that you can with the help of God give that gift to others.

For a complete list of resources by Ray Comfort, visit **LivingWaters.com**, call 800-437-1893, or write to: Living Waters Publications, P.O. Box 1172, Bellflower, CA 90706.

NOTES

1. You can view our movie "Crazy Bible" freely at tinyurl.com/wlayldk.
2. Alexia Fernandez and Liz McNeil, "Why Doris Day Will Have 'No Funeral, No Memorial and No Marker': 'She Didn't Like Death,'" *People*, May 13, 2019.
3. "What is the meaning of I AM WHO I AM in Exodus 3:14?" GotQuestions.org <tinyurl.com/rhoxe8s>.
4. C. H. Spurgeon, "The Peacemaker," delivered December 8, 1861, at the Metropolitan Tabernacle, Newington.
5. C. H. Spurgeon, "The Uses of the Law," delivered April 19, 1857, at the Music Hall, Royal Surrey Gardens.
6. C. H. Spurgeon, "The Cleansing of the Leper," delivered December 30, 1860, at the Metropolitan Tabernacle.
7. C. H. Spurgeon, "A Private Enquiry," delivered October 9, 1890, at the Metropolitan Tabernacle, Newington.
8. "Matthew 19–Jesus Teaches on Marriage, Divorce, Riches, and Discipleship" <enduringword.com/bible-commentary/matthew-19>.
9. John Sinnott, "Israel Folau sacked following anti-gay social media post," CNN, May 17, 2019.
10. C. H. Spurgeon, "The Peacemaker," delivered December 8, 1861, at the Metropolitan Tabernacle, Newington.
11. C. H. Spurgeon, "The Question Between the Plagues," delivered May 4, 1885, at the Metropolitan Tabernacle, Newington.
12. Charles Wesley, "And Can it Be That I Should Gain? " 1738.
13. C. H. Spurgeon, "God's Law in Man's Heart," delivered June 28, 1885.
14. "Guide Me, O Thou Great Jehovah," words by William Williams, 1745 (p.d.), *The Methodist Hymnbook* (UK), 1933.
15. Jamie Ducharme, "Stephen Hawking Was an Atheist. Here's What He Said About God, Heaven and His Own Death," *Time*, March 14, 2018.
16. Ibid.
17. Ibid.

18. Ibid.

19. George Eaton, "Richard Dawkins interview: 'I'd rather people read my books than my tweets,'" *New Statesman*, January 30, 2019.

20. C. H. Spurgeon, *Morning and Evening*, "Evening, January 12."

21. "Almost Half of Practicing Christian Millennials Say Evangelism Is Wrong," February 5, 2019 <barna.com/research/millennials-oppose-evangelism/>.

22. Ibid.

23. Michael Foust, "Ten Commandments No Longer 'Applies to Us,' Says Popular Megachurch Pastor," Christian Headlines, January 10, 2019.

24. Albert Einstein, *Einstein on Cosmic Religion and Other Opinions and Aphorisms* (New York: Dover, 2009), p. 97.

25. Compendium of the Catechism of the Catholic Church <tinyurl.com/jfuwl>.

26. John Bunyan, *The Pilgrim's Progress* (Buffalo: Geo. H. Derby and Co., 1853).

27. "Dunning–Kruger effect," Wikipedia <tinyurl.com/ch94y5w>.

28. Dennis Prager, "The Worst Sin," December 23, 2014 <dennis-prager.com/worst-sin>.

29. "What does it mean to take the Lord's name in vain?" Got Questions.org <tinyurl.com/tcs5qoq>.

30. "Sunday: 'As His Custom Was,'" Sabbath School Net, April 25, 2015 <ssnet.org/blog/sunday-as-his-custom-was>.

31. "The Disciples Kept the Sabbath 85 Times in the book of Acts" <eliyah.com/85times.html>.

32. Logan Strain, "5 Murders Committed For Mind-Blowingly Stupid Reasons," CrimeWire, October 15, 2013 <tinyurl.com/rcvblfp>.

33. Will Maule, "Progressive Scientist Describes Staggering Change of Heart on Abortion," FaithWire, May 28, 2019 <tinyurl.com/usbdo75>.

34. C. H. Spurgeon, "The Prodigal's Return," delivered February 7, 1858, at the Music Hall, Royal Surrey Gardens.

35. Alexia Fernandez, "Actor Isaac Kappy Dead After He 'Forced Himself Off' a Bridge and Was Hit by Car," *People*, May 14, 2019 <people.com/movies/actor-isaac-kappy-dead>.